THE ULTIMATE BABY BOOK FOR NEW DADS

THE ULTIMATE BABY BOOK
FOR NEW DADS

100 WAYS TO CARE FOR YOUR BABY IN THEIR FIRST YEAR

Roy Benaroch, MD

Illustrations by Jeremy Nguyen

ROCKRIDGE
PRESS

Interior and Cover Designer: Stephanie Sumulong
Art Producer: Hannah Dickerson
Editor: Shannon Criss and Samantha Holland
Production Editor: Ashley Polikoff
Illustrations © 2021 Jeremy Nguyen, except for the following: © Christian Dellavedova, pp. 17, 32-33. Author photo courtesy of Kelley Wenzel, Pear Tree Photography.

ISBN: Print 978-1-64876-628-2
eBook 978-1-64876-132-4
R0

For Dad.

CONTENTS

An Introduction to Dadhood: How to Use This Book

You're a dad! Well, maybe not yet. But if you're reading this, I'm guessing you will be soon. The "cover charge" to get into this club wasn't steep. But now that you're in, I know you've got questions. Your first one might be, "Can I do this?"

Yes, you can! You've got it in you. I've been a practicing pediatrician and a dad of three kids for more than 20 years. I've coached thousands of new parents, and I promise that you really don't need to know much before getting started. What you do need is love and the drive to do the right thing for your children. A little curiosity and a sense of humor help, too.

My first child was born 22 years ago while I was a pediatric resident. I was a doctor in training, and I had delivered, held, and cared for babies, but never one of my own. Taking care of children was my job. But I wondered: How would I have the energy to do this *and* be a dad, all the time, forever?

Then, my daughter was born. I held her, and it all made sense. Having your own baby is not a job. It is who you are. You're a dad, all the time. And you know what? It's the most rewarding and fun thing you could ever be.

As I mentioned, you don't need to know much to get started. But there is plenty to learn! Your most important and lasting lessons are what you learn from your own child. What do they like, and what makes them tick? I'm a pediatric expert, and I've gotten to know thousands of children. But you're going to become the expert on your own child. That's a crucial and unique role.

Our babies depend on us for their health and safety. But they also need us to provide an enriching home to help them grow and discover the world. It's amazing, really. At first, our babies only watch, listen, and cry or fidget when they need something. But soon, they learn to smile and laugh, too. They'll copy your facial expressions, sharing your smile when you see a friend or pouting when you decide not to give them a cookie. Babies then become master explorers and scientists, getting into everything they can reach and attempting small experiments to figure out how the world works: "Does this fit in my mouth? What does Dad do when I put spaghetti on my head?"

In this book, I'll travel alongside you as your companion and guide. My advice is based on my own experiences and the best and most up-to-date scientific information. You'll learn about your baby's growth and development, both physically and mentally, including what you should expect and how you can help. Discussions will also include information about daily routines, feeding, and nutrition, as well as the importance of having an ongoing relationship with your child's physician, whether they are a pediatrician or family medicine specialist. The physician will get to know your child well and will be a great resource for specific questions and concerns. You'll want to schedule regular checkups, including growth and developmental assessments and routine vaccinations, to make sure your child stays healthy and safe.

Welcome to the club, Dad! Let's do this!

FROM HEAD TO TOE

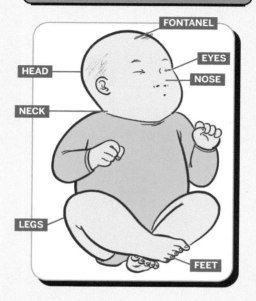

To start off, let's take a look at some of the basic parts and functions of your newborn.

Head: Your baby's head is relatively large, and the birthing process can cause bruising or squishing.

Eyes: They are often puffy at first. Your baby's eye color will change as your baby grows.

Nose: Sometimes flattened at first, your baby's nose is small and might sound congested.

Hair: It can be a variety of colors and thick, thin, or curly. It may fall out after birth, but don't worry. It will grow back.

Neck: A baby can't keep their head up yet, so support it when lifting them.

Fontanel (soft spot): This area is protected by tough fibrous tissue that will eventually be replaced by bone. You can touch there—it won't hurt.

Body: To fit inside the uterus, your baby has been rolled up for months! Now your baby will want to stretch out.

Legs: A young baby's legs may appear bowlegged.

Feet: Some baby feet are blue at first; that's a normal part of newborn circulation.

Skin: Baby skin is often peeling, like a snake's. Birthmarks are common and can mean different things. Discuss these with your baby's doctor.

Color: Your baby should look pinkish, though the shade depends on family skin tone. A bit of yellow (jaundice) is usually no cause for alarm.

Genitals: Boys have a small penis, with the expected scrotum and testicles nearby. A girl's external genitals are her vulva. The vagina is inside.

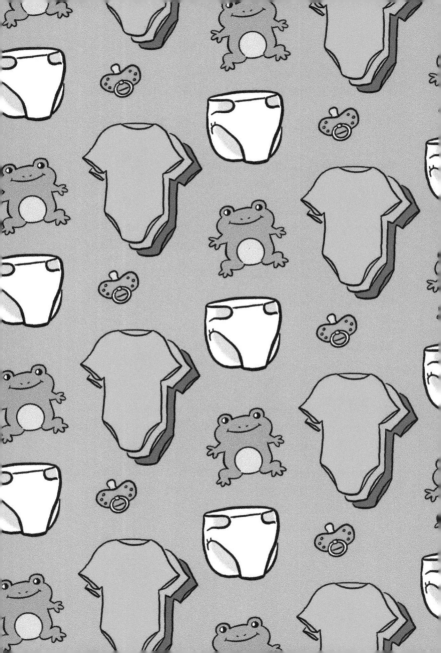

CHAPTER 1

0 TO 3 MONTHS

It's time to get started! This period of your child's development is hard to visualize. Your life will change. Days and nights can run together, and your sleep will be interrupted. You should be there for both your baby and your partner. They're working hard, and they're not sleeping much, either. So be kind and don't worry about getting everything perfect. Your home will get cluttered, and laundry will not get done. That's okay.

In some ways, this can be a calm and peaceful time. There will be some crying and fussing (all babies need to blow off some steam), but most of the time, your child will be either asleep or quiet and awake, wanting to be held while they look around. Help them feel loved and safe. Your baby won't expect much active play yet. Feeding might seem a little monotonous to you (milk again?!), but for your baby, breast milk or commercial formula is what they need to thrive. Your exact daily schedule may be unpredictable. You can make plans and will more or less be able to count on a certain cycle as the days go by, but your baby gets the "final vote."

GROWTH AND DEVELOPMENT

During this time, you're going to hear the word "milestone" a lot, but I don't like that word. It makes people think of set markers: one mile, a chunk of stone that declares exactly where your baby ought to be. But babies move at their own pace, sometimes lurching ahead or falling behind. It's all progress.

There is a lot of research on the changes to expect as babies grow. Though there are no precise targets, most babies hit most of their anticipated milestones around the expected time. Don't feel disappointed if your baby seems a step behind in one or two areas. Embrace who they are, and marvel at every step. Your baby will only grow up once! In this book, you'll learn about things you can do to gently nudge your child along. If you have misgivings about how your baby is growing or learning new skills, it's best to discuss them with their doctor.

Mental Development (Vision & Hearing)

At birth, your baby can see but can't adjust their focus, so the image they see will only be sharp for faces or objects about 8 to 10 inches away. By two months, your baby will want to focus on your face. By three months, they'll be able to use their eyes to track a moving object. Occasional eye crossing is fine in young babies.

In the U.S., most states require a hearing screening for newborns to identify babies who might need extra help.

Your child should be able to hear well from birth, though they won't be able to localize, or tell what direction a sound is coming from, yet.

Physical Development (Movement & Growth)

Newborns always lose a little weight at first, but your baby should be back to their birth weight by about two weeks. After that, they'll gain about an ounce a day for the next few weeks and three to four ounces per week after that.

Early limb movements might not be smooth or coordinated, but from birth, your child should be able to move all of their limbs and their head symmetrically, or in all directions. Sometimes there might be a little tremble or shake. Strength comes quickly! By three months, babies can often push or lift their head up and can briefly hold up the weight of it.

THE ROUTINE

Getting into a routine can be tricky at first, so don't try to force one. Just nudge your baby toward a routine that is already developing. If your baby naps at about the same time for a few days in a row, aim to start tomorrow's nap at that same time. Although you can't sleep train a baby this early, you should reinforce good habits to set the stage for later success. Put your baby down while they are still awake, at least sometimes. Try starting the next nap after quiet awake time or playtime rather than right after a meal. Prepare for a firmer routine that you can develop over the next few months by aiming for consistent meal-times and naptimes and by using consistent and safe locations for most sleep.

Dr. Knows Best: Sleeping on Their Own

At first you will find that your baby sleeps best in your arms. That's okay. It's sweet and feels warm and snuggly. But you should also put your baby to sleep in their crib or bassinet sometimes. Give them a chance to learn to sleep on their own so sleep training is easier later on.

CHECKUP SCHEDULE

A crucial part of every checkup is "anticipatory guidance," or discussing what to expect and how to handle upcoming challenges. Checkups are also great opportunities to get your questions answered, so bring a checkup list.

→ **3 to 5 days of life:** Some practices call this a "weight check," others a "full well checkup."

→ **2 weeks:** Many practices perform a full checkup at two weeks. By this time, your baby's weight should be back to their birth weight.

→ **1 month:** Repeat the physical exam, making sure growth and development are on target.

→ **2 months:** Start building and strengthening your baby's immune system with the recommended vaccines.

FEEDING & NUTRITION CHART

Until four to six months of age, most babies only need breast milk, commercial baby formula, or a combination of the two. No extra water is needed. When mixing baby formula, use the exact recipe on the packaging. It's usually fine to use ordinary municipal tap water to mix formula.

All breast milk–fed babies should receive a daily vitamin D supplement.

The following table shows typical volumes for bottle-fed babies. Of course, you can't measure intake when babies nurse. Nursing babies who have had enough usually become sleepy or disinterested in taking more.

NEWBORNS	1 TO 2 MONTHS
After the first few days of life, newborns typically take 2 to 3 ounces per feeding.	About 4 to 5 ounces per feeding

Generally, young babies take about two and a half ounces per pound of body weight per day. To compare the daily amounts consumed, add up ALL of the feedings across several days and average them out.

POSTPARTUM SUPPORT

"Postpartum" means "after birth" and traditionally lasts about six weeks. If your partner gave birth to your baby, it can be an especially tough time, with a lot of (sometimes unspoken) questions: "What have I done? What am I doing?" You can help your partner best by:

Talking. It's okay to ask these questions out loud. Tell your partner you're in this together, things will get better, and that they're doing an amazing job.

Doing. Get your hands dirty. Help with the legwork: laundry, cooking, shopping. Plan nights where you stay up to let your partner sleep.

Understanding. Help your partner understand that you both have mixed feelings. You might be irritable, sleep-deprived, and snappy with each other. You both have a lot on your plate, and it will help if you carry the load as a team.

Asking. You'll need extra help. Solicit real, hands-on assistance from family, friends, or neighbors to help with dishes, run a few simple errands, or do laundry. (You will be shocked just how much laundry an eight-pound baby can generate.)

Protecting. Shield both yourself and your partner from unhelpful advice and unhelpful visitors. A lot of people will be eager to tell you what you are doing wrong. You and your partner do not need to hear that right now.

Providing. Your partner will really appreciate your making sure there's plenty of one-handed food around (bagels, apples, cheese, maybe a granola bar that includes chocolate). Help out with meals by shopping, organizing, picking up takeout, or cooking—it doesn't have to be fantastic, and it will be appreciated!

POSTPARTUM DEPRESSION

Mild symptoms of anxiety or depression are sometimes called the "baby blues." Mood swings and irritability affect up to 85 percent of postpartum women (and many men, too). These symptoms typically last a few weeks and improve with sleep and support. Feelings of sadness and worry are common and normal, and it's okay to feel this way.

But sometimes, issues are more severe and pervasive, including sadness or withdrawal; feelings of worthlessness, guilt, shame, or restlessness; and trouble concentrating or sleeping. If these symptoms overwhelm you or your partner, last longer than a few weeks, or if there are thoughts of self-harm or harming your baby, contact your physician immediately.

There's an elevated risk for significant postpartum mental health concerns among people who've had previous anxiety or depression and those with poor social support. A baby's own temperament can make this period more difficult. Some babies are more anxious and fussy, contributing to a cycle of worry and worsening sleep.

Postpartum depression or anxiety can be rough on a family, and you can't treat it alone. Don't delay seeking treatment. With help, it gets better. Often, treatment includes some combination of talking with a therapist, working with a support group, and taking medication that's safe for nursing women.

BABY MASSAGE

Giving your baby a massage can be fun and relaxing, and there's evidence that it can help with motor development and sleep. Follow these steps to give it a try. (Don't forget to offer your partner a massage, too.)

1. **Pick a quiet time that's not right after a feeding.** Some families like to do a massage at the same time each day as part of a soothing sleep routine.

2. **Pick a calm place.** Choose somewhere you can sit or stand comfortably with your baby.

3. **Talk and explain.** Your baby loves your voice. Say, "It's massage time," talk about what you're doing, or sing a soothing song.

4. **Get naked!** (Your baby, I mean.) You can leave on a diaper. Or take a chance if you don't mind cleaning up your baby's clothes or the carpet later.

5. **Stroke or massage each body part.** Be gentle but firm; this isn't a tickle. Start with your baby's head, neck, and shoulders; then move to their back, thighs, knees, and hands. Every part should get 30 to 60 seconds of your attention. You'll also want to move and gently stretch your baby's neck and extremities.

6. **Pay attention to your baby.** They might not like certain positions. Do more of what's relaxing for both of you. If some parts of the massage don't go well or your baby doesn't seem to be in the mood for it, try again later.

7. **Consider using oil or lotion.** Try cocoa butter. It's a great moisturizer that smells like chocolate.

SLEEP GUIDELINES

Volumes of research have contributed to guidelines for the best and safest baby sleep environments.

Babies should be put down to sleep on their backs (see illustrations on page 11). Once your baby can roll over on their own, you don't have to *keep* them on their back all night, but it's best to put them down that way. Don't use positioners, wedges, straps, or anything else to keep babies in a certain position, because they're just not safe.

The sleep surface should be firm, flat, and horizontal (not inclined). Here are a few other tips:

→ There shouldn't be soft or loose bedding, bumpers, or toys around. These can entangle a baby, leading to possible suffocation.

→ Do NOT use an inclined sleeper, car seat, or bouncy seat for routine sleep. They're not safe and have caused deaths in infants.

→ Never place your baby on a couch, sofa, or armchair to sleep. If your baby does fall asleep in one of these, move them to a safe place.

Your baby can share your bedroom but should have their own separate sleep surface (like a crib or bassinet). Only bring your baby into your bed for comfort or feeding, and then return them to their own sleep surface when they're sleepy. The American Academy of Pediatrics (AAP) does not recommend bed-sharing or co-sleeping (see page 24).

Don't rely on products that claim to help monitor your baby or keep them safe. These devices haven't been evaluated as medical devices, and there's no evidence that they help.

SLEEP INDUCEMENT

You might think that falling asleep is easy or automatic, but it's not. Babies need to *learn* how to fall asleep. You can't force it, but you can set the stage to make it easier. As with any other skill, some babies are faster than others when it comes to learning how to fall asleep. Whether you've got an easy sleeper or a kiddo who fights sleep, the following tips for good habits are the same:

Be gentle. Quiet, slow, relaxed holds and shushes can help.

Pay attention and learn your baby's cues. Some babies yawn when they're tired, others pass gas or rub their eyes.

Be consistent. Choosing similar times each day and a similar place and setting can help build mental cues that tell your baby it's time to sleep.

Don't wait until your baby is overtired. If you wait until your baby is very sleepy, they'll be too strung out and upset to make a smooth transition. Start your sleep routine *before* you think your child is really tired.

Consider using a pacifier or white noise machine. Some babies find these relaxing.

Try swaddling. This helps best for babies from newborn through about two months of age. Not all babies like a swaddle, but many find it relaxing. Safe swaddling allows the legs to move freely (see page 32).

INFANT CONSTIPATION

Your baby's poop pattern changes dramatically in the first few months of life. At first, they may poop four or more times a day, almost every time they nurse or take a bottle. That slows down considerably around four to six weeks, especially for breastfed babies. After that, your baby may poop only every few days or even once a week.

How do you know if your baby is constipated? It's all about consistency. A baby who's passing soft and squishy poop, even just once a week, is not constipated. A constipated baby will pass firm or solid stools, sometimes resembling little pebbles.

Don't be fooled by grunting or the faces your baby makes. Sometimes, there's a big show as babies figure out how to push while relaxing their anus to let stool pass. Grunting and turning red isn't constipation unless the poop is hard.

If your baby is constipated, make sure you're mixing your formula with the correct amount of water. Talk with your baby's doctor before adding extra water or offering fruit juice. These common remedies must be used carefully with young babies. You can also help your baby relax by offering a gentle massage while "bicycling" their legs.

BOTTLE PREPARATION

Commercial baby formula is safe and provides good nutrition for your baby. Although it comes available in liquid concentrate and premixed versions, most families use the powdered versions because they're more affordable. You'll just have to do the legwork to mix them up correctly.

Use clean bottles, nipples, and mixing containers. They don't need to be sterile or boiled. Just wash or run them through a dishwasher between uses.

Use ordinary tap water. If you're not sure if your tap water is safe, you can boil it for one minute and let it cool before use. Bottled water is acceptable, but it's not necessary.

Follow the mixing instructions *exactly*. Add a measured amount of water directly to a bottle or a mixing container, then add one level, unpacked scoop of formula powder per two ounces of water. Use the scoop that comes with the package of formula. Shake well to mix.

Use the prepared formula immediately, or keep it in a refrigerator for up to 24 hours. Formula left at room temperature should be discarded after one hour. Don't reuse any leftovers in a bottle after your baby's had a meal.

It's traditional to mix and use baby formula warmed up, but warming isn't required. Many babies quickly get used to room temperature or even chilled formula. If you want to warm up premade formula, the best way is to float the bottle in hot water. Test a bit of the formula on your own skin to make sure it's not too hot.

Dr. Knows Best: Which Formula Is Best?

There are many different formulas available, making it hard to know which is best. Ordinary cow's milk–based formula from any manufacturer works great for almost all babies, whether using it alone or as a breast milk supplement. Most of what distinguishes these different formulas are catchwords and labeling, not actual or meaningful differences in what they contain or their nutritional value. They're all pretty much the same, so use what works best for your baby.

BURPING BABY

Becoming a champion burper may not have been on your bucket list before fatherhood, but there's something satisfying about helping your baby bring up a noisy burp. You'll develop your own style. Here are some steps to get started:

1. **Set the stage.** Burping isn't just about air. Often something wet comes up, too. If you like your shirt or your carpet, you might want to have a "burp cloth" or towel handy.

2. **Be gentle.** You cannot force a baby to burp. Gentle taps or rubs on their back work well, or maybe a few (soft) whaps with a cupped hand.

3. **Find a position that works.** Different babies prefer different burping positions. Holding the baby up on your shoulder with their face over your back works for some. (I did mention having a burp cloth ready, didn't I? Sling it over your shoulder first!) Or, you can place your baby facedown on your thigh or facedown across your forearm. You'll find your baby's most effective burp position soon enough. (See the illustrations for some ideas.)

4. **Relax and talk.** Your baby, especially at first, might find the odd sensation of a burp coming up scary or uncomfortable. You can help dispel their fear by talking gently or even joking about it. "Wow, that's a big one" or "Let's get that bad boy up" are appropriate comments.

5. **After a while, stop trying.** Most burps will come up in a few seconds or maybe half a minute. If you're trying for more than a minute, it's time to quit. Burping your baby is traditional, and it does seem to help babies settle, but it is not essential. Sometimes, no burp will come up, and that's okay.

OVER THE SHOULDER

THE FOOTBALL

THE LAP OF HONOR

BREASTFEEDING SUPPORT

Many breastfeeding parents find it easy and enjoyable once Mom and baby get the hang of it. At first, there's almost always some pain and uncertainty, and it may take practice. Here are some great ways for dads to help support a breastfeeding partner:

Help with the little things. Soothing, bathing, changing, and holding are all important parts of nursing. Yes, only Mom can nurse, but there are lots of ways to pitch in. Help your partner look for signs that your baby is hungry or ready for feeding.

Protect your partner. Avoid having too many visitors at the beginning of your nursing journey. Get help from a few trusted friends or relatives, a lactation specialist, and your baby's physician.

Be encouraging. Your partner is most likely tired and may be questioning her abilities as a new mom. Tell her you're proud, that she's doing a good job, and that you can see how difficult it is.

Keep an eye on the big picture. Stay in touch with your baby's physician. Nursing is great, but sometimes things don't work out as planned. There are many healthy options, including pumping and formula supplementation. The bottom line is to keep both Mom and baby physically and mentally healthy so they can enjoy each other.

POOP STUDY

Baby poops come in various shapes and colors. A different color or consistency is usually nothing to worry about. Here are some ordinary stool types:

Meconium: This poop happens in the first few days. It's black to dark green, thick, sticky, and often difficult to wipe off.

Newborn poop: After about four days of life, once the meconium is "washed out," newborns poop several times a day. The color is usually yellow—sometimes more greenish or brownish—with "seeds" of curd. The consistency is soft like applesauce.

Baby poop: This yellow to brown poop appears around one month. It's less frequent, sometimes just every few days (less frequent in breastfed babies). It has a consistency like toothpaste and puts off a more "adult" odor.

Overall, the color of poop doesn't matter much. Anything along a green-yellow-orange-brown rainbow is fine. But there are some colors that should prompt you to contact your baby's physician:

Red or black: This might be blood. Sometimes, it's from a fissure on the outside, or it could be from inside the baby's gut. It could even be swallowed blood from Mom's breast.

White: Poop should have some color—from green to yellow to brown—from bile acids secreted from the liver. White or colorless stool may indicate a liver problem.

DIAPER CHANGE

Change your baby's diaper whenever there's stool or more than a little moisture. Since most families use disposable diapers, here are the steps for changing those, but there are other options.

1. Never leave a baby unattended on a changing table! Keep one hand on your baby the whole time. They're squirmy and may surprise you.

2. Use a location that doesn't strain your back. After all, you're going to be changing a lot of diapers.

3. Be prepared with wipes (and extra wipes), spare diapers, diaper cream, and a hygienic place for disposal. A baby wipe warmer is not necessary.

4. Tell your baby what you're doing, or sing a diaper-changing song.

5. Get all clothes out of the way, including your baby's socks and your necktie.

6. "Unbuckle" the diaper straps, but don't pull the diaper off yet. With the soiled diaper in place, use wipes to sweep the stool into the soiled diaper. If there's just urine, only a brief wipe is needed. You might have to lift up your baby's feet with one hand to get everywhere.

7. Wrap the old diaper around the used wipes and toss it in a diaper pail (designed to be hygienic and reduce odor).

8. If you're feeling brave, have some naked time and dry that bottom with a fan. If you're feeling extra-crazy brave, dance with your baby on your head like a hat (hold them with both hands).

9. Replace the diaper, dress your baby, put your baby down, and wash your hands. Repeat as needed.

HANDLING WITH CARE

Babies aren't as fragile as you might think. They do not break easily, and you shouldn't be afraid to handle them. Here are some dos and don'ts for handling your baby:

DOS	DON'TS
Hold and cuddle your baby.	Don't shake your baby. Never, ever, ever.
Provide extra neck support, especially for babies less than a few months old. When you pick them up, put one hand behind your baby's head.	Don't pull hard on your baby's arms or legs. Don't swing your baby around.
Change wet or soiled diapers frequently.	Don't toss your baby. Throwing your young child (gently) in the air is a fine pastime and will get you laughs when your child is older. But now is not the time. Besides, you'll get puked on.
Touch and massage your baby.	
Gently move their limbs around, while talking and explaining what you're doing.	Don't worry too much about the fontanel, or soft spot, on the head. It's a myth that you shouldn't touch it. You can. It's covered with tough fibrous tissue, and you won't hurt your baby by touching this area.
Be careful while cooking or around hot water.	
Gently nibble on your baby's ribs or neck while making chomping noises. Around three months old, they find this hilarious.	Don't worry about conversation, laughter, and (reasonably) loud noises. You can run a vacuum, and you can listen and dance to rock music with your baby in your arms.

SKIN-TO-SKIN

Skin-to-skin time was first popularized for nursing moms as a way to soothe babies, enjoy quiet bonding, and help with stress and milk production. It turns out that skin-to-skin contact is a great idea for all parents: dads and bottle-feeding moms, too. It helps build your confidence and can help your baby feel soothed, warm, and protected. Some studies show skin-to-skin time leads to less crying and a decreased release of stress hormones for parents *and* babies.

Typically, skin-to-skin time is done with your baby naked (or wearing a diaper), lying facedown with their tummy on your bare chest. You'd usually place a blanket over you both, not covering your baby's head. You can wrap your arms around your baby if you'd like. You can talk or tell stories, sing or hum, or just enjoy a few quiet moments.

Remember: This position is not for sleeping. Babies shouldn't be put to sleep on their front or while lying on an adult. When it's sleep time, place your baby on their own separate surface, faceup (see page 10). If your baby does fall asleep on you, move them to a safe place.

CO-SLEEPING

Co-sleeping is when parents and their children share the same bed. Recent guidelines based on studies of unexpected infant deaths have shown that co-sleeping increases risk, especially in young babies. The American Academy of Pediatrics (AAP) does not recommend co-sleeping. It's best if your baby only comes into your bed for feeding or bonding time while awake. If your baby does fall asleep in your bed, move them to their crib or another safe sleep surface.

This recommendation has led to a lot of heated discussion and disagreement. *Most* cases of deaths of babies while in a parent's bed have been associated with multiple other known risk factors: babies less than four months of age, babies born small or premature, smoking in the household before or after pregnancy, parental use of sedating drugs or alcohol, or co-sleeping, especially on soft bedding or a couch, sofa, or armchair. There is also an increased risk if any adult in the bed is not the baby's parent or is overweight.

Critics of the AAP's stance against co-sleeping point out that co-sleeping makes breastfeeding easier and promotes bonding. But babies who sleep in their parent's bed have a higher risk of death. Though that risk can be reduced, it can't be eliminated.

CO-SLEEPING MYTHS

Guidelines that discourage co-sleeping may seem controversial, in part because of persistent myths that appear in popular media. But here's the honest truth:

Myth: Babies who die while co-sleeping *always* have other risk factors.

Truth: Most babies who die during co-sleeping have multiple risk factors, including co-sleeping. With no other risk factors present, co-sleeping multiplies the risk of death by three, though the absolute risk remains small.

Myth: Parents can't make co-sleeping safer.

Truth: For parents who really want to co-sleep, there are ways to reduce (but not eliminate) the risk. Avoid soft beds or bedding, and never co-sleep on a couch. Do not smoke or take any sedating drugs or alcohol. Make sure your baby doesn't overheat and don't overbundle them. Always place your baby down to sleep on their back. Make sure all vaccines are up-to-date. And consider waiting until the peak time for sudden infant death syndrome (SIDS) has passed (four months after birth).

Myth: Deaths from co-sleeping are common.

Truth: About 3,500 infants die each year in the United States because of unsafe sleep (including bed-sharing and other factors). A study from the United Kingdom that separated out the various contributors found that the risk of death of a co-sleeping baby with no other risk factors was 1 in 16,400. However, with multiple risk factors present, this risk increases to as high as 1 in 150.

LAUNDRY TIME

A newborn baby weighs about six to eight pounds. Even after a few months of life, we're talking about 15 pounds of baby, max. But the amount of laundry that little one can create is truly impressive. Here are some tips and tricks for a dad who's ready to do his part:

Stay ahead of the game. Don't be surprised if—thanks to swaddle blankets, burp cloths, onesies, and bedsheets—you need to do laundry every day. If things do turn into a big pile, remember that the way to wash a mountain of clothes is to start shoveling.

Believe in the presoak. There are a lot of choices and home remedies for stain removal, but a great trick is to presoak with some extra detergent.

Scrape off whatever "yuck" you can. Before tossing the clothes in or near the hamper, scrape off any semisolids. You know what I mean.

Stay away from heavily scented detergents. You don't have to buy an overpriced "special for baby" laundry detergent, and you also don't need one that smells like the Canadian wilderness. Your two-month-old is not a Mountie yet.

Don't overstuff the washing machine. You will be tempted. It won't work out well.

Put those tiny socks in a lingerie bag. Use a mesh bag with a zipper to wash delicate or tiny things without your washing machine tearing them to bits. Otherwise, you will never see those little socks again.

Buy inexpensive clothing. When your baby's clothing gets hopelessly stained, you won't feel so bad about tossing it out.

Dr. Knows Best: Beginning Tummy Time

Babies should always be put down to sleep on their backs for safety (see page 10), but they need to exercise the muscles in their chests, too. Practice "tummy time" when your baby is awake, starting when they are only a few days old. Put your baby facedown on their tummy. Stay nearby to talk to and encourage them. Just a few minutes a few times a day works better than one long stretch. If your baby starts to fuss, pick them up and try again later.

TAKING PATERNITY LEAVE

Paternity leave can be a great time to get to know your baby while also helping out your partner. Depending on your employer and where you live, you may have multiple options.

In the United States, federal law under the Family and Medical Leave Act (FMLA) provides for up to 12 weeks of unpaid leave for fathers after the birth or adoption of a child. This doesn't apply to everyone or to every employer. For instance, you must work at a location with 50 or more employees, and you must have worked for the same employer for 12 months. As they say, other exclusions apply, and your employer may insist that you use up your paid or vacation time first. Many states have additional laws and regulations regarding both paid and unpaid leave, often called "family leave" or "parental leave," that sometimes apply to moms and dads. Other countries have paternity leave policies that are more generous.

Talk with your employer about your plans and expectations. You probably won't know the exact date of your baby's birth in advance, so you'll want to come up with a flexible plan for your transition and coverage no matter how long you plan to be out. Many companies support family leave over and above what's required by law. It never hurts to ask for more information.

LISTEN TO THE HEARTBEAT

Many of us first heard our baby's heartbeat at an obstetric or midwife appointment, listening to the flow of blood through the Doppler ultrasound. It's more of a swish than a thump, but it is truly the heart's rhythm. For many, it's the first time that a new life seems real.

After your baby is born, take a few minutes to listen to their heartbeat. Until the mid-1800s, physicians listened to hearts by pressing their ear against a patient's chest. But you can easily learn to use a stethoscope—either borrowed or purchased—yourself.

1. Choose a quiet time. (You cannot hear the heart well in a screaming baby. That's an advanced pediatrician skill!)

2. Place the stethoscope ear tips in so they face forward, and hold the head of the stethoscope right in the middle of your baby's chest, directly against the skin. Try not to move it around.

3. Listen. Can you pick out the two tones, the "lub" and the "dub"? They're faster than you might expect. A young baby's heart rate, even while asleep, is often more than 100 beats per minute. If you listen for a while and watch their chest, you might pick out something subtle; the normal heart rate varies with breathing, speeding up as babies inhale. You may also hear each breath. During a whole life span, a human heart beats over a billion times.

DIAPER RASH

Think about what baby skin has to put up with: spit-up, drool, poop, urine. These are irritating, and trapping them against the skin is asking for trouble. Fortunately, most diaper rashes can be prevented or treated.

To prevent diaper rash: Change diapers as soon as possible when wet or soiled. Allow the skin to dry completely (use a fan or the cold setting on a hair dryer). If you have time, leave the skin naked to the air for a minute or two. If your baby gets frequent diaper rash, use diaper cream before putting on a clean diaper.

To treat diaper rash: Follow all of the instructions to prevent diaper rash. You want plenty of cool, dry, naked time. And start using a diaper paste or cream with every change. Most diaper creams contain zinc oxide mixed in petrolatum to create a soothing, waterproof barrier. (This includes brands like Desitin and Balmex, as well as generics.) Don't be stingy when there's a rash. Buy diaper cream in a big one-pound tub and apply it with two fingers after you put on a disposable glove (or it will get all over you and under your nails). With the next change, clean up the bottom and add more cream to the skin.

If your baby's rash isn't responding or seems severe, or if your baby is acting unwell, contact their pediatrician for additional advice.

Dr. Knows Best: Elimination Communication

Diapers are the main cause of diaper rashes because they trap stool and urine against the skin. There is a different way to prevent diaper rash called "elimination communication." Essentially, this is a way of raising babies without diapers at all by paying attention to their cues and the timing of their bowel and bladder habits. It is not for everyone, and it is not the same as potty training, but some families find it helpful. For more information, see Resources on page 180.

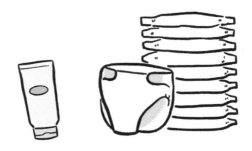

THE SWADDLE

Many young babies and newborns find swaddling soothing, perhaps because it re-creates the tight feeling of being in the womb. If you'd like to try to swaddle your baby for soothing or sleep, follow these tips:

→ Keep your baby's hips and legs loose. A good, safe swaddle holds the upper body fairly tight but allows free movement of the lower limbs.

→ Always place your swaddled baby down to sleep on their back.

→ Stop swaddling when your baby tries to roll over, typically around two months of age.

And here are the steps to properly swaddle your baby:

1. Place a blanket down in a diamond shape with the top corner folded toward the center. A fabric with a little spring to it works well. Place your baby on the blanket with their shoulders over the fold, so their head isn't on the blanket.

STEP 1

2. Hold your baby's right arm straight down while folding over the left side of the blanket, tucking it under your baby's opposite side.

3. Loosely pull the bottom of the blanket up.

4. Now hold the baby's left arm down and wrap the extra blanket from the right side up, over, and around the opposite shoulder. It can be a little tight, but don't go crazy; you should be able to slip a few fingers under the blanket. Make sure your baby's hips and legs are loose and mobile.

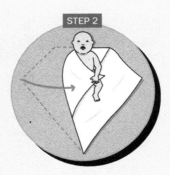

There are special swaddling blankets available with Velcro-style straps that make these steps easier. Avoid using one that limits the motion of the legs or holds your baby's upper body too tightly. A swaddle isn't meant to be super binding or firm.

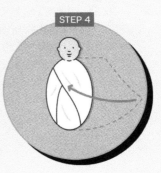

BATHING BABY

For the first few weeks (until the umbilical cord stump falls off), give your baby sponge baths. You can do baths every day or a few times a week. The key is to set everything up before you've got a slippery baby on your hands.

1. Choose your bathing spot. The kitchen sink works great. Since the counter is higher than your bathroom sink or tub, it's easier on your back. The sink hose attachment (if you have one) works for rinsing, too.

2. Gather your bathing items: a baby bathtub to sling over the sink, a soft washcloth and towel, and some gentle baby soap. Have a clean diaper and a set of clothes handy.

3. Set your water heater to no more than 120 degrees Fahrenheit and feel the water to make sure it's luke-warm to warm and comfortable. Keep a hand on your baby at all times; they're slippery and squirmy!

4. Baby skin doesn't need to be scrubbed, but you can gently rub to get your baby clean. Start with their face, rinse as you go, and do their butt last. Don't forget the folds and crevices behind ears, between toes, and behind knees. As always, talk and explain as you go, or sing a bath time song.

5. Rinse well, gently pat dry, and enjoy your warm and good-smelling baby!

QUICK-CHANGE ARTIST

Baby clothes get icked up quickly, and sometimes at the worst moments. No matter how clean your baby started out, things get messy.

Keep a few spare sets of clothes handy. You should also always have spare wipes and a few plastic bags (both for tossing soiled diapers and for keeping or discarding dirty clothes).

Make sure the spares are easy-on and easy-off. Some baby clothes have frills and extra flaps and things. When you're in a hurry, simplicity counts.

If you can't use your usual changing table, sometimes the floor is best. You know your baby can't roll off the floor. When you're in a hurry, pick a place that's super safe.

Disposable wipes are wonderful. Sure, you can use wipes to clean your baby's bottom, but you can also use them to get spit-up out of a baby's neck folds or do other quick cleanups. In a pinch, a handful of wipes can replace an entire bath.

Remember, safety first. Your cleanup doesn't have to be perfect, and your baby doesn't have to be dressed in matching clothes. Get the soiled stuff off, clean up a bit, and throw on the new clothes while keeping one hand on your baby. Don't worry—you'll get better at this with practice.

BABY FEELS: THE TEXTURE OF YOUR FACE

By the time your baby is about a month old, they will become very interested in your face, especially your facial expressions. Babies figure out that we communicate our moods and what we're thinking with our expressions and our mouths and our eyes. And they'll want to learn to do it, too. Work on building your baby's early communication and exploration skills with these steps:

Help your baby explore your face. Lean close and hold their little hands. Help them touch and feel your nose, cheeks, chin, lips, eyes, whiskers—everything.

Explain what they are touching and feeling. For example, "This is Daddy's big nose," and take a big sniff, and "This is Daddy's mouth, for eating and chomping" (feel free to accompany this with chomping noises or pantomime). You could also say, "That's Daddy's chin. It gets scratchy at the end of the day," or "That Daddy's lower lip. It's soft!" Your baby will want to feel your hair, eyebrows, and ears. Keep talking and telling stories about each part (what your eyes do, what your ears are for, etc.).

Take turns. Feel the soft texture of your baby's face, the squish of their cheeks, and the soft cartilage of their ears. You can even do some fortune-telling: "Someday, your chin will get scratchy like mine," or "Someday, you're going to meet someone that makes your heart beat fast, and your eyes will get really big like THIS!"

THE BENEFITS OF BONDING

Bonding builds positive physical and emotional changes for you and your baby. While bonding, babies experience less stress and more organized sleep. Dads, moms, siblings, and other caretakers become more confident and happier as a result. Rocking, singing, talking with eye contact, and holding your baby close helps them feel loved and secure. These feelings can set the stage for building trust, friendships, and relationships later in life.

Bonding is a constant, ongoing process. There is no single crucial time for bonding. Sometimes medical issues or other things come up at first, but that doesn't mean that bonding isn't going to occur. It may just happen differently from how you imagined.

One crucial element to bonding is responsiveness. Pay attention to your baby, and your baby will pay attention to you. Look out for cues and noises, and talk about what you and your baby are doing. Feel free to joke around and be yourself ("Hey! I make that noise sometimes, too!").

Bonding is not competitive, and your baby has an infinite capacity to bond with others. The more, the better. No matter who else is holding or caring for your baby, you will always be special. Only you are Dad.

EXPLORING REFLEXES

Infant reflexes (sometimes called "newborn" or "primitive" reflexes) are preprogrammed body movements that originate in the brain stem. They're present at birth, and "extinguish," or disappear, over 2 to 12 months. (The exact timing depends on the reflex, with variability among babies.) Checking these reflexes is an important way for your child's doctor to monitor their nervous system and development. Eliciting these reflexes takes practice, and you might not get all of them to appear every time. Here are some examples of your baby's reflexes and how to find them:

Rooting: When you touch your baby's cheek or the corner of their mouth, they'll turn their head and open their mouth to that side.

Moro: Also called a "startle" reflex, this happens when a baby is startled by a loud noise or sudden movement. They'll throw back their head, extend their arms and legs, and then pull their limbs back in.

Tonic neck: When you turn your baby's head to the side, the arm on that side stretches out while the opposite arm folds at the elbow, like the position of a fencer.

Grasp: Stroking the palm makes the fingers grasp. This works on feet and toes, too.

Stepping: Try holding your baby upright, then lower their body until their feet touch a surface. They'll take a few "steps" or seem as if they are dancing.

Galant: With your baby's face held down, facing away from you, gently stroke the sides of their back. Their spine will curl toward your stroke.

VISITING YOUR BABY'S DOCTOR

Heading for a trip to your child's pediatrician? Here are steps to follow so you can get the most out of your visit:

1. If this is your first visit, bring your hospital paperwork. Yes, it should have been faxed to your doctor or (even better) be accessible via direct computer interface. That doesn't always happen, so come prepared.

2. You're probably tired and have a lot of questions. It's a good idea to bring a list of the most important things on your mind so you get the answers you need.

3. Pack your bag with spare clothes, diapers, wipes, and plastic bags. Many doctors stock these at their offices, too. We've got you covered.

4. If your baby is using a pacifier, bring it. If you're bottle-feeding, bring bottles and spare formula. Babies get impatient for their snacks.

5. If the doctor offers ways to "pre-check-in," like completing forms online or printing them and filling them out in advance, do it. It saves time, cuts down your wait, and gives you a chance to complete these materials carefully and accurately when you're less rushed.

Pro tip: Babies sometimes make funny movements or noises that puzzle parents, but then they don't do them in front of the doctor! If you're concerned about something like this, try to bring a video. Sometimes a simple photo of a fleeting rash can help, too.

> ### Dr. Knows Best: Vaccines Are Crucial
>
> *Along with good nutrition and a loving home, the most important thing you can do to keep your children healthy and safe is to get all of their recommended vaccines on time and on schedule. My children got them, and your children should get them, too. Pediatricians know they work and that they are safe. When you have questions, please check with your child's pediatrician and reputable science-based resources.*

HELPING YOUR CRYING BABY

All babies cry, some more than others. Sometimes their crying means something: maybe they're upset or they need something (food, a diaper change, etc.). Other times, babies cry to let off steam or frustration. Many babies cry more in the evening. This "normal crying" peaks at about six weeks of life, trailing off by the third month.

Here are some steps for your "crying action plan":

1. Check if your baby needs something. Are they warm or cold? Is their diaper wet or soiled? Are they hungry? Did their foot pop out of the leg of their jammies?

2. If nothing in step 1 seems to fit, go into soothing mode. You know your baby is okay, but they need reassurance. Here are some ideas to try, alone or in combination. You'll learn what works best for your own baby.

   → Hold your baby and walk around using a rocking motion. Some babies want to be held upright, some prefer facing downward across your arm.

   → Offer a pacifier. Many families find these helpful, and they won't cause problems with nursing.

   → Swaddle your baby (see page 32).

   → Buy a white noise generator. This is much easier than going "shush, shush, shush" over and over.

3. The most crucial step: Take turns with your partner. It may be time for a handoff!

Rarely, excessive crying can be a sign of a medical issue. If you think your baby is crying too much, make an appointment with your baby's doctor for an exam and discussion.

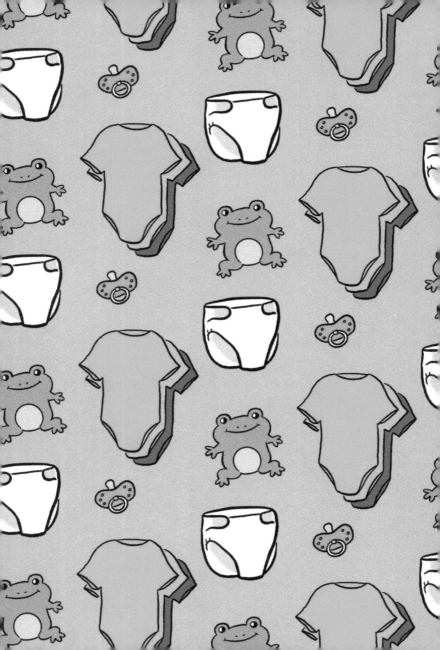

CHAPTER 2

4 TO 6 MONTHS

Welcome to "the golden age of babyhood." Your newborn was adorable, and you've had time to bond and watch them grow. This next phase is more fun. Your baby is smiling, probably laughing, and has even started to "talk." (Don't expect to make much sense of their words just yet. It's a work in progress!)

During this stage, you need to be physically and mentally there for your baby and partner. The work doesn't let up. In some ways, babies become more demanding of time and attention as they develop more interest in the world around them. Your baby will want to do more than watch you or stare at toys. They will want to be a part of your life.

By now, your daily schedule may have become more predictable and routine, but there will still be surprises. Your baby will start to eat solids, which means more messes and more stinky diapers (more on that later). This chapter delves into your new schedule, your baby's expected growth and development, and how you can help your baby thrive. You've gotten your feet wet already, and now it's time to dive in!

GROWTH AND DEVELOPMENT

It's amazing how different your baby is from a few months ago. They're much more interested in the world, recognizing familiar faces and starting to acknowledge their own name. They'll begin trying to tell you things. For example, they'll reach toward you to communicate, "Pick me up!" Pay attention to those cues to reward your baby, and have fun together!

Years of research have given pediatricians a good understanding of the way babies grow and develop. But every baby is different, with some babies jumping ahead in certain areas while others are a bit slower to develop. All babies strive to learn new things and new skills. Be nurturing and supportive, but not pushy, and resist the temptation to compare your child with other kids their age. If you're concerned that your child may be behind in their development, see your pediatrician for an evaluation.

Mental Development (Vision & Hearing)

By around four months, your baby should see in full color and have vision in the 20/40 range. Babies at this age prefer to see people up close. Their world—what they're most interested in—is your face and immediate surroundings.

Around four to six months, babies start to localize sounds. They'll turn their head toward new or interesting noises. They'll also respond to the tone of your voice and might be frightened by loud or unexpected things. The beginnings of speech emerge, too, with sounds like "aaah" and "ooooh."

Physical Development (Movement & Growth)

In past decades, most babies would have learned to roll over by four months old. That's no longer true. Babies now spend more time on their backs for safer sleep, and they can easily see you without having to flip over. Don't worry, significant later milestones (such as sitting up and walking) have not been pushed back. Rolling over is now typically learned by six months. Four- to six-month-olds can hold their heads up, sit up with support, and kick or press their feet down to "dance."

Around four months, many babies will have doubled their birth weight and will continue to gain about one pound of weight and one-half to one inch of length every month.

THE ROUTINE

As your routine develops, think about your child's needs and your schedule. Are you a morning person? Do you or your partner work firm hours? Does your baby like a few long naps or several shorter catnaps? Almost any routine can work, but consider nudging your baby toward a consistent schedule, typically anchored by meals and a fairly rigid bedtime. Try feeding right when your baby wakes up. Here's a schedule you can start with and modify as needed:

7 a.m.: Wake up, eat, then play

9 a.m.: Naptime

10 a.m.: Wake up, eat, then play

12 p.m.: Naptime

1 p.m.: Wake up, eat, then play

3 p.m.: Naptime

4 p.m.: Wake up, eat, then play

5 p.m.: A solid meal (try new things)

6 p.m.: Bath time (tip: do this right after solid meals)

7 p.m.: Meal (breast or bottle), then bedtime routine

Dr. Knows Best: Make Your Own Schedule

Your baby's schedule mostly depends on you. Do you and your partner like to keep a predictable schedule? Or do you crave spontaneity? Your baby gets a vote, too. You'll learn quickly if you've got a baby who does better with a firm routine. Either way is fine—what's best is what works for you and your family.

CHECKUP SCHEDULE

Your baby should have a routine checkup (sometimes called a "well check," "wellness visit," or "health maintenance visit") at both four and six months. Try to schedule these on time because the timing of the routine vaccinations at these visits is important. You want your baby to get the best protection, and you don't want to make extra visits to catch up.

As always, the second most important thing to bring along with you is your checkup list—the key questions you want to ask. (The first most important thing to bring is your baby, but you probably won't forget that.)

FEEDING & NUTRITION CHART

Most of your child's nutrition from four to six months should be from breast milk or commercial baby formula. Typically, a baby takes six to seven ounces from a bottle or nurses five to six times a day.

BREAST MILK	BABY FORMULA
It's best to nurse 5 to 6 times a day.	6 to 7 ounces of formula, 5 to 6 times a day.

You'll want to start solids (or complementary foods) between four and six months for experience, fun, and allergy prevention. Never put cereal or anything other than formula or pumped milk in baby bottles.

A few other things to remember:

→ Babies who nurse or take a mix of breast and bottle with less than 16 ounces of formula a day should receive a vitamin D supplement of 400 IU daily.

→ Extra water isn't necessary, unless the weather is really hot. For practice, you can give a little water from a sippy cup with solid meals.

PROPER DIAPER DISPOSAL

An average baby—and while I'm sure your baby is above average, let's stick with average here—goes through about 2,000 diapers during their first year. Babies fly through diapers even more quickly during the first months. Most parents prefer to use disposable diapers, but there are other options available, such as cloth (wash-and-reuse) diapers. The following instructions are for safely discarding disposable diapers.

1. **Dump solid contents into the toilet and flush.** Not everyone does this, but it is better for the environment to keep solid waste out of landfills.

2. **Wrap used wipes in the diaper.** Then, wrap the diaper into a ball, using the straps to secure it. This helps reduce odor.

3. **Seal it up.** You can use a commercial diaper pail contraption like a Diaper Genie, which makes a string of sausage-like garbage bags, or you can tie diapers up in grocery or zip-top bags.
4. **Toss the bagged diaper into the garbage.** It's best to discard the diaper outside, or at least into a can that's emptied frequently, such as one near the changing table that's designated specifically for diapers. If you're at a friend's home, ask where to discard the diaper. If you're out and unsure where to throw away the diaper, consider double-wrapping it and carting it back to a hygienic disposal place. Most offices, understandably, do not want diapers tossed into their trash (except pediatricians—we expect it!).
5. **Wash your hands.** You were probably careful, but wash them anyway. Use hand sanitizer only in a pinch, and then wash your hands as soon as you can. Nothing beats soap and water.

PACKING THE DIAPER BAG

A diaper bag can be a backpack, a soft-sided duffel bag, or anything that's sturdy, easy to carry, and has enough pockets and nooks so everything is organized. You'll want a separate compartment for soiled or wet things.

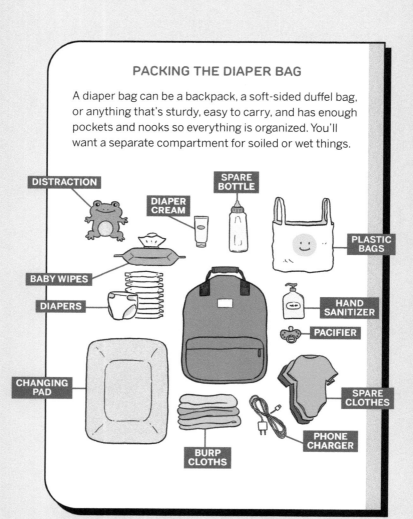

DISTRACTION

SPARE BOTTLE

DIAPER CREAM

PLASTIC BAGS

BABY WIPES

DIAPERS

HAND SANITIZER

PACIFIER

CHANGING PAD

SPARE CLOTHES

PHONE CHARGER

BURP CLOTHS

Here are a few items you'll want in your diaper bag:

- **Diapers:** Bring twice as many as you think you'll need. As your baby grows, replace the unused ones with diapers of the right size.
- **Plastic bags:** These are for tossing soiled diapers and bundling up wet clothes. You can reuse grocery bags or use zip-tops.
- **Spare clothes:** Carry at least two sets of easy-to-change outfits (typically onesies, but whatever you prefer) and swap these out as your baby grows.
- **Baby wipes:** These are usually in a small, portable container.
- **Hand sanitizer:** It's better to wash your hands with soap and running water after changing your baby, but sometimes that's not possible.
- **Extra burp cloths:** These clean spit-up and work as all-purpose towels, washcloths, butt cleaners, changing pads, or even as a comforting lovey.
- **A changing pad:** Waterproof is best, so nothing leaks through.
- **Diaper cream:** Prioritize if your baby has sensitive skin or is prone to rashes.
- **If your baby takes bottles:** Pack a spare (plastic) bottle and either a small factory-sealed container of ready-to-feed formula or a portioned amount of formula powder.
- **Extra pacifiers:** If your baby uses one.
- **A toy (distraction) for baby** and a phone cord/charger for you.

CREATE A NICKNAME

My own nickname, used well into my adult years, was "Tiger" because I mewed like a baby tiger as a newborn. Some nicknames stick and some don't. Here are some ideas to think about for your little one:

Pick one that can last. "Boo" or "Little One" might lose its luster as your child ages.

Build on their given name. Robert can be "Rocky" (as in Balboa!). Michael can be "Mickey." Josephine can be "Joey," "Jojo," or "Josie."

Build on a last name. Use your last name or your partner's last name or maiden name, as appropriate. Smiths can be "Smitties." If your child's name has a title (Junior, Third, Fourth), how about "JR," "Trip," or "Trey"?

Some initials flow right off the tongue. Maybe you've got a JP or an RB? Or an LA can be spoken as Ella. You can use first and last initials, first and middle initials, or all three pronounced together.

Base it on family or baby stories. These can also be incorporated into a nickname. One child in my practice was born before they made it to the hospital on McAlister Street, and he's been called "Al" ever since.

Give your child veto power. They might insist you call them something different when they're old enough to develop their own opinion. And your partner gets a vote, too. Don't get too invested in one name, and try to find something everyone can be happy with.

OVERCOMING TENSION: DEFUSING DISAGREEMENTS

You and your partner won't agree on everything, and disagreements can become even more explosive when you're sharing the responsibility of raising a baby. Remember, you're from different backgrounds, and you weren't raised the same, yet you both turned out okay. Often there is more than one right answer.

To work through disagreements, it can help to try to see the other side. Repeat what your partner said in your own words. Did you understand them? In the long run, being able to listen and appreciate each other's viewpoint is much more important than being right.

Sometimes it can help to put an argument on hold or just sleep on it. It could be that the next day you're more amenable to compromise on what you had disagreed about. You might even discover you weren't disagreeing at all, you just didn't understand your partner's point of view.

I'll share with you a bit of wisdom my own dad shared with me the day I got married: Don't sweat the small stuff. There will be times when you will disagree with someone you love, and sometimes the best decision you can make is just to drop the issue. This isn't about winning, losing, scoring points, or being right. It's about two exhausted people making it through the day together, raising a child, making each other happy, and sharing a laugh or two. It doesn't do any good to win a fight and go to bed angry.

TUMMY TIME

Tummy time helps your baby develop chest and arm muscles and gives them an opportunity to learn to roll and look at the world a different way. Not all babies like tummy time. It feels different, they're not used to the position, and they can't see you. If your baby gets upset, feel free to end the session early. Here are some examples of fun tummy time activities:

→ Start tummy time when your baby is fed (but not too full!) and in a good mood.

→ Stay nearby where your baby can see you. Put your face down at their level. That's what your baby wants to see.

→ Get down on your own tummy so your baby can see and imitate you.

→ Lift your baby up like an airplane, complete with noises and swoops, but don't be surprised if you get burped on.

→ Go chest to chest. You can do tummy time lying on your back with your baby facedown on your chest.

→ Entertain and distract them with songs, imitated voices, and funny faces. How's that Donald Duck voice coming along?

→ Take a walk with your baby facedown across your forearm. You can explore your home or go outside. Keep talking while your baby tries to look up and see what's going on.

→ Gently practice rolling by helping your baby get halfway there.

→ Add toys to the mix. Something like a ball or colorful stuffed animal to reach for can be fun.

→ Keep tummy time brief. Multiple short sessions a day are better than one long one.

OUTSIDE PREP: ALL SEASONS

Getting outside means being prepared. *Almost* any weather is fine. If you'd want to go outside, it's probably good for your baby, too.

Cold weather: Dress your baby in about as many layers as you're wearing, and bring extras just in case. Avoid anything tight or stringlike around the neck, including woolly hats that tie underneath. Mittens are better than gloves. Babies have relatively large heads that lose a lot of heat, so add a warm hat when it's cool.

Warm or hot weather: When it's warm, a simple onesie is enough. Direct sunlight might be hard on a baby's eyes, so walk in the shade on bright days. You can buy baby sunglasses, but they won't always stay in place. Make sure you have sunscreen, if needed (details on page 59).

Rain and snow: Think about safety here. You don't want to slip while carrying your baby, and you don't want the stroller to go careening away. You also need to stay visible to vehicles. If visibility is poor, or you're not sure you can stay on your feet, stay inside. If you head out in the rain or snow, bring a rain cover for your stroller, an extra layer for your baby, and a blanket for tucking around them to keep them warm.

PREVENTING SUNBURN

For babies younger than six months, it's best to avoid sunburn by staying out of the sun when it's directly overhead at midday and using clothing and big hats to cover exposed skin. When good shade and full-covering clothing is impractical or unavailable, you should use sunscreen on exposed skin at any age.

Aim for a sunscreen that's at least SPF 15 (ideally higher) and provides broad-spectrum protection. Spray-on sunscreen might seem easier to apply, but it goes everywhere and it's difficult to use on small, squirmy babies. It's usually better to buy a cream that stays where you put it.

There's some concern about certain sunscreen chemicals that may accumulate in the blood, like oxybenzone and other ingredients with similar-looking names. It hasn't been proven that they're harmful, but if you want to be extra careful, stick with sunscreens that include only the active ingredients titanium dioxide or zinc oxide. These are not absorbed into the body and are safe for any age.

BABYWEARING

Babies are more than just a fashion accessory. Wearing your baby while you're out can help you stay connected and give you an opportunity to explore the world with your child. You might even find that it eases some everyday activities, like chores and shopping.

There are various ways to wear your baby. Slings are most suitable for young babies. Or find a contraption that holds your baby upright in front of your chest, either facing backward or forward. (After about four to five months, they'll prefer facing forward so they can see what's going on.)

Whatever style carrier you use, you'll want to wear your baby safely. It should fit your baby fairly tightly and keep them upright, but it shouldn't be too snug. You should be able to slip your hand in between your baby and the carrier; if you can't, it's too tight.

You'll be walking around with your hands free, so the baby carrier itself needs to hold your baby securely in place. Their head should be close to your face (close enough to lean over and kiss) with the head supported, if necessary, so their chin doesn't fall down to their chest. Your baby's back should also be supported so they don't scrunch down in the carrier. There are several brands and shapes of carriers, and you might need to try a few to find one that fits your baby's shape and your physique correctly and comfortably.

Dr. Knows Best: Playing Rough

It's fun to engage in physical play with your baby: holding them on your head, bouncing them, lifting them up high. But don't get carried away. Between four and six months isn't the time for tossing your child in the air or swinging them around. Active play is okay, but your baby isn't a professional wrestler. If you do like to play a little rough, pay attention to the reaction. If your baby doesn't seem to be enjoying it, stop.

VISUAL STIMULATION

One way your young baby explores the world is through vision. You'll see how big their eyes get when they see something (or someone) new and interesting. To a baby, the world is full of things to explore, so give them plenty of new visual adventures. Check out the following ideas:

→ Change the scenery by moving the crib's position in the room. Put your child down on their back in different positions, facing different ways.

→ Offer reach, touch, and grab toys or mobiles. Chunky and colorful wooden or plastic blocks are great, too.

→ Carry your baby while walking around the room or neighborhood, talking about what you see. Your baby should be exposed to things that are near and far, indoors and out.

→ Show them what you're looking at and touching: your shiny keys, your phone, your hamburger. Talk about the colors, what things look like, and what they're for.

→ Play games like patty-cake while holding and moving your child's hands where they can see them.

GOING FOR A DRIVE

It's time for your first long trip with your baby. This could be an hour or more in the car to visit Grandma or to check out a traveling carnival. Here are some things to keep in mind when planning a longer trip:

If possible, take a comfortable and large vehicle. Someone will probably sit in the back with the baby. You also need room for the diaper bag, backup outfits, and luggage. Pack more than you think you'll need.

Use teamwork. The driver must stay focused on driving, so someone else should stay in the back for baby's entertainment. You may want to tag team and trade spots.

Take breaks. Unexpected and unplanned breaks will happen. Enjoy the scenery and find a small park to explore.

Plan ahead. Bring your pediatrician's contact information and any medicine your child might need. If your child has special health care needs, ask ahead of time where you might be able to seek appropriate urgent care.

Strap your baby in. Some babies object to their car seats either right away or after being strapped in for a while. Regardless, don't give in. There's no negotiating this point. When your vehicle is moving, your kiddo must be strapped in. If they're hysterical, park and let everyone take a break.

CAR SAFETY

The single most important safety feature in your vehicle is the driver. Stay focused on the road. Don't fiddle with your phone, and don't try to watch or steal a glimpse at your baby. If leaving your baby alone facing backward makes you anxious, bring someone else along for the ride to sit with them in the back. Here are some other safety tips:

- Use a new car seat, or one you are 100 percent sure has not been in an accident.
- Make sure your car seat is fitted correctly to your car. Your local police or fire station can help if you're unsure.
- Make sure your baby is fitted correctly for their car seat.
- The best position for your baby is backward, in the middle of the back seat.
- Don't use mirrors or other contraptions to help the driver see the baby. They're distracting.
- Always have your baby strapped in when your vehicle is in motion or when there are other cars moving nearby (like during carpool drop-off).
- You shouldn't routinely have your baby sleep in a car seat for long periods of time. If they do fall asleep in the car seat, move them to a safe, flat sleeping surface once you get where you're going.

DISINFECTING TOYS

Baby toys are germ magnets. Don't let babies share them. Bring your own baby toys wherever you go, especially to the pediatrician's office. Try to keep them clean by washing or sanitizing them daily or whenever you notice they're sticky or dirty. Expect that your baby's toys are going to spend a lot of time in your baby's mouth. Here are a few tips on selecting toys and keeping them clean:

Choose toys that are easy to clean. Plastic toys should be able to go through a regular dishwasher cycle. If you don't have a dishwasher, clean off visibly soiled  areas with a soapy washcloth, and then spray down the toy with a disinfecting solution or wipe. Rinse with clean water.

Cloth toys and stuffed animals should be machine-washable and dryable. If they're small, put a bunch together in a lingerie bag before tossing them in the washing machine.

Some toys are trickier.
Toys that plug into an electrical socket or contain batteries can't be submerged or run through a dishwasher, so you'll have to rely on disinfecting wipes or solutions (be sure to rinse them, too). And toys that have a rubbery texture might not do well with the heat of the dishwasher. Avoid any toys that are a hassle to clean.

Avoid toys that have paint that may chip off, stickers, or crevices that will be impossible to clean. If a toy is just getting too "well loved" to clean, throw it out and buy a new one.

BABY STROLLS

Getting outside with your baby is a great idea. You could both use a change of scenery, and to a baby, a trip around the block is filled with new sights and sounds. A baby stroll might include the whole family and even the dog. Or you could leave your partner at home so they can enjoy a break. If you're having a rough evening with a fussy baby, splitting the work helps. Offer to take a soothing walk with the little one while your partner recharges.

You'll want a good stroller, but you don't have to spend a fortune. Some convertible strollers transition from backward-facing for younger babies to forward-facing for around six months, when babies become more interested in the outside world. Alternatively, a wrap, sling, or infant carrier that straps to your body works well. It depends on your style and what your baby likes.

Although sunshine helps your baby make their own vitamin D, you should avoid the heat during the middle of the day. If it's superhot or crazy-cold outside, it may not be the best day for a walk. Wait for a day when you and your baby will be more comfortable.

During your walk, talk to your baby. Explain the sights and sounds, or just talk about what's on your mind. It's good practice for when your child is older. Hearing your voice and seeing your face are among your baby's favorite "hobbies." Get into the habit of talking with and listening to your children.

CLASSIC PEEKABOO

Peekaboo is an important developmental game that helps teach your baby that separation from their loved ones doesn't have to be scary. Cultures around the world have played peekaboo-style games with babies for hundreds of years. The following are a few variations you can try:

→ Keep it light and funny. Use silly voices and a smile.

→ Do very brief "disappearances" at first, and then work up to making them just a little longer.

→ Vary the way you or your child "disappears." You can briefly hide yourself, covering your face with your hands or ducking down behind furniture or around a corner. Or you can cover your baby's eyes with your hands, your baby's hands, a towel, or toy.

→ When you hide, it's traditional to say, "Peekaboo," but feel free to change it up. Appropriate comments are "Where's Daddy?" or "Daddy's gone!"

→ When you reappear, say, "I see you!" But, again, follow your heart and mix it up. "Here's Daddy!" or "I'm baaaack!" works well, or even "Heeeeere's Johnny!"

→ Frequent short sessions are best. When you repeat the game over and over, your baby will start to anticipate what happens next, and you'll get big belly laughs.

→ Don't forget to crank up the silliness! Pair up with your partner and "reappear" as them and vice versa (this takes a bit of timing practice, but some kids just love this trick), or pop back up with a silly face or a funny mask.

THE NIGHT SHIFT

By four months, about half of all babies sleep through the night. Maybe you got lucky and you've got a great sleeper already. Other babies have a hard time getting to sleep. Sleep is one of those things, like eating and pooping, that you cannot *force* your baby to do. But you can nudge your baby toward longer stretches of independent sleep.

The most important step is having a bedtime routine. With newborns and young babies, parents often get in the habit of holding or rocking them to sleep. But that could pose a developmental problem. Soon, babies become aware of when you or your partner have snuck away. You put them down all comfy and asleep, but when they realize you've left, they're scared and need you back. A baby who's put down after falling asleep in your arms is going to have a difficult time falling asleep again later when they're on their own.

By the time your baby is four to six months old, you should usually put your baby down awake. Your baby needs to learn how to fall asleep independently. This doesn't always work at first, but keep trying. Be confident and loving. If they cry, wait a few minutes before picking them up and work on lengthening that pause every few days. It's worth it for you, your partner, and your baby to get a good night's sleep. Read more about this on page 86.

SLEEP DEPRIVATION: FATHER'S EDITION

Parenting young babies is an exhausting 24/7 job. You and your partner may not have gotten a good stretch of sleep in months, and that can wear you down physically and mentally. Here are some tips to help you get through:

Take turns. Assign some nights for one or the other of you to stay in bed, no matter what. Use a white noise machine or fan to drown out sounds that keep both of you up, or plan to have one partner sleep closer to the baby so the other person can sleep.

Take a mini-vacation without your baby. This may not be practical for nursing moms, and some families may not feel ready for this yet. But if your child has grandparents, they'd probably love to take care of them for a few days while you and your partner recharge.

Don't overdo caffeine or alcohol. These beverages might seem to help in the short run, but too much of either will prevent restful sleep and may worsen symptoms of mental illness.

Beware of anxiety or depression. These interfere with sleep and health. If you or your partner is having problems beyond the ordinary, seek professional help.

DAY CARE SELECTION

There's a lot to consider when choosing day care, including questions about affordability, location, and your own personal preferences. You'll want to visit your candidates more than once, at different times of day. Spend a little time watching to get to know their routine. It can also help to network in your neighborhood. Here are a few specifics to evaluate:

→ **Safety:** Make sure that safe sleep guidelines are always followed and that every baby remains visible at all times. (For example, cribs must be see-through and arranged so they don't block each other.)

→ **Accreditation:** Licensing is required by each state, but that's a fairly minimum standard. To better ensure quality, look for a day care that's been nationally accredited.

→ **Cleanliness:** There's going to be clutter, and that's fine. Remember, these are kids! But you shouldn't see grime, mold, or old food.

→ **Infection control:** Day cares should require all recommended vaccines and should have a strict sick plan that keeps ill children and staff home. Handwashing or sanitizing stations should be easily accessible and used frequently. Ask what happens if a child gets sick during the day.

→ **Interaction:** Young babies need close, personal, one-on-one attention. The American Academy of Pediatrics recommends a staffing ratio of no more than three babies per one adult caretaker for day cares catering to babies less than 12 months of age. The caretaker should be spending a lot of time holding and playing with babies down on the floor.

Dr. Knows Best: Infections Happen, Day Care or Not

Babies who start group care as infants may seem to get more infections at first, including more coughs, more runny noses, more fevers, and more GI bugs. But large studies have shown that, in the long run, these kids aren't any sicker than children who weren't in day care. In fact, children who first join group care settings in kindergarten get more colds that first year than children who've had previous exposures.

INTIMACY WITH YOUR PARTNER

Every aspect of your life changes after childbirth, and that includes your sex life. It's important to be open and honest with your partner. With a new baby in the house, you may have to change your expectations.

That being said, the relationship between a baby's parents is just as important as the relationship with your baby. You must nurture your adult relationship. Part of that is taking the time to enjoy your romantic life.

There will be a lot on your minds. Gently pull your attention back to you and your partner when your baby is asleep or in little snippets with romantic texts or moments throughout the day.

You and your partner are most likely really tired, and that can kill an intimate mood. Flowers or chocolate are great, but helping your partner get a good nap or a solid night's sleep may be a better aphrodisiac.

Physical changes also come with having a child. If your partner is a nursing mom, she is going to have low levels of estrogen and may find vaginal sex dry or uncomfortable. Don't be embarrassed or disappointed. Lube will help solve the problem. Your partner's body is still changing and might be shaped a little differently than before she had the baby. Maybe yours is, too. Dads can sometimes gain weight during pregnancy, and you may not have been hitting the gym as regularly. Sex is about love, and it should be fun. It doesn't have to be perfect every time.

SEX REEDUCATION

Sex after birth can be extra fun, if you let it. You may have to sneak sex in or steal a precious moment for it. But there are some common myths that can ruin the mood:

Sex should start six weeks after birth. This "rule of thumb" isn't based on science. Some people will be ready for sex sooner, and some later. Be patient. Sometimes, it's the partner who didn't give birth who wants to take it slower, and that's okay, too. Couples who adopt may find that their changing family affects their sex life as well.

Nursing moms can't get pregnant. This is a myth. Use birth control, or expect a surprise.

The vagina is loose after childbirth. There are changes, yes. Whatever changes occur with childbirth often resolve with time, and sometimes simple exercises can help. If your partner is experiencing pain or feels there's been an unwanted physical change, have her talk to her doctor.

Sex will never feel as good. You might feel awkward or tentative at first, or scared that someone will get hurt. In time, your sex life can be just as good as it was before. Don't worry about timelines or expectations. You can get the groove back.

DANCE!

Dance, sounds, and music are essential for babies to learn motion and self-control, and they are all fun ways to enrich your baby's life.

Choose tunes that appeal to your own style. Your baby doesn't require "baby music." Listen and dance to what you like and what you want to share with them.

Select different tunes for different moods. Try Simon & Garfunkel to fall asleep or Beastie Boys to clean up toys.

See what your baby likes or what they're in the mood for. Tell them about the music you've put on and why you like it.

Move! Move your arms, wiggle your neck, shake that behind. Your baby will be watching and soon copying your moves.

Try an instrument like maracas, a drum, or a kazoo. Choose something unbreakable that your baby can play, too.

Add sound effects. It's time for some beatboxing, and not just the percussion parts. Sing the lead guitar's solo, or add parakeet squawks or a fire engine siren with your own voice.

Hold your baby's hands. With your baby sitting in front of you, hold their hands (or feet!) while going through your dance moves together.

Hold your baby *in* your hands. Give your baby a spin in your arms as you sing. Swing it (but not too hard)!

Repeat. Babies love repetition, and quiver with anticipation when they know what's coming next. So come up with some of your own signature moves at certain times during your favorite song. You might swoop your baby down low, or raise them up high, or combine a move with a kiss or an "Oh, yeah!" Your baby will learn to expect it and love it.

ENCOURAGING SOUNDS

A baby's communication skills blossom between four and six months, including their having more interest in sounds. Your voice, environmental noises, and your baby's own vocalizations are fascinating to them. Speech and communication starts with listening, mimicking, and responding to sounds. There are lots of fun things you can do to encourage these skills:

Talk with your baby. Look them in the eye and talk with them like a friend. Include pauses for them to respond. They won't respond every time, but that's coming soon!

Pretend to understand your baby's early speech. True, their coos and noises aren't making sense yet, but baby is trying. When your baby says "Gaaaa," you could say, "You're right, Grandma is coming over," or "Yeah, I don't like that wallpaper either," or "That's a good point, they're drawing the goalie too far out." Then wait for their response and answer again.

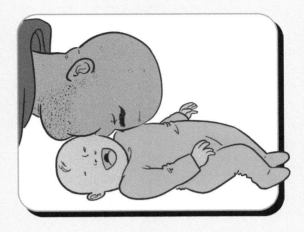

Blow raspberries. Linguists call these "bilabial fricatives." They're important for speech and oral-motor development, and your baby will soon learn to copy it and laugh. Spit bubbles are fun, too, but maybe not in front of Grandma.

Imitate other nearby noises. The microwave oven signal, the doorbell, the dog's whining, the noise at the end of the washing machine cycle, etc., are all part of your world, and your baby will soon learn what they mean.

Sing! It doesn't matter how melodic your voice is. Your baby will love your singing. Bonus points for including hand gestures or an improvised dance. Your baby will learn from those, too.

CHECKING IN WITH YOUR MENTAL HEALTH

A lot has changed. You have a growing family, new routines, new roles for you and your partner, and a huge new responsibility with a baby. You may be wondering, what does the future hold? Are you doing the right thing? Have you already blown it? Every dad has these questions. But if they're weighing too heavily on your mind, you may be at risk for developing a significant mental illness, which can adversely affect you, your baby, and your partner. You owe it to yourself and your family to check in: How are you doing, Dad?

These are some warning signs that may mean you need further evaluation. Any of these conditions might occur briefly, to some degree, with a new child, but if any are persistent or pervasive, you should seek help:

→ Big changes in your sleep patterns or appetite

→ Losing touch with your own personal care

→ Not enjoying your usual hobbies, friends, and interests

→ Thinking illogically

→ Significant lapses in memory or concentration

→ A decreased ability to do your work or study

→ Irritability or flying off the handle too easily

→ Moodiness, getting stuck in one negative mood, or having rapidly changing moods

→ Becoming apathetic or disinterested

→ Excessive anxiety or worry that interferes with things you enjoy or prevents you from getting things done

→ Paranoia or worry about things that are unreasonable

→ Feeling a "lack of reality" or a disconnection from the real world, like you're watching your life instead of living it

→ Any thoughts of harming yourself or others

Dr. Knows Best: Exercise as Medicine

There is one treatment that's effective for almost every symptom of mental illness: vigorous exercise. Exercising regularly can help anxiety, depression, apathy, lack of energy, insomnia, or lack of concentration. I know that when you're feeling down, it's hard to start. But once you do, you'll feel better. Don't worry about how much exercise you do or whether you do it regularly or if you're out of shape. Get moving and you'll feel better.

YOUR PARTNER'S MENTAL CHECK-IN

Although postpartum depression usually begins before four to six months after giving birth, your partner is still at risk. Lack of sleep, body changes, and worries about a new baby, careers, and finances can leave your partner stressed out. Here are some ways to support your partner's mental health:

Stay connected. You are a team. Sometimes you might "divide and conquer" your chores, but make sure you're also doing things together.

Communicate. Take the time to talk and actively listen to what your partner is saying. Ask follow-up questions. See how things change and what solutions work or don't work.

Set aside time specifically for the two of you. Your baby is important, but so is your relationship. Grandparents can help, or a sitter, or a neighbor. Maybe you can trade off childcare with neighbors for a few hours. Make it happen.

Look for warning signs of more serious issues. Help your partner get evaluated by a mental health provider if needed. Pervasive sadness, withdrawal, disinterest, anxiety, or a big change in personality or functioning are red flags you need to look for and take seriously. Sometimes, mental illness can manifest in physical symptoms, like headaches, abdominal pain, or dizziness. Don't assume its nerves or baby blues. Get these symptoms checked out by a physician.

MIRROR BABY'S MOVEMENTS

Babies learn from watching, listening, and copying. They learn the "conversational volley," or talking back and forth, by speaking during your pauses, and they figure out how to feed themselves by watching you put food in your mouth. Babies copy the noises you make, your speech patterns, and your body language.

Many of the emerging skills from four to six months are in the motor realm, or learning to move muscles in a coordinated, goal-oriented way. This skill takes practice, and that's where "mirror movements" come in. You can help reinforce your baby's developing skills by showing them, through your movements, exactly what they're doing with their body.

It works like this: Your baby should be facing you, so you're easy to see, preferably in a neutral or upright position. Start mirroring your baby's movements, so they see in you exactly how their limbs move. Copy their facial expressions, and move your body the way they're moving. You can reinforce this for extra bonus points by explaining and talking, too. For example, say, "I'm grabbing for my beard," or "What's my foot doing here?"

You can make this a little more complicated by introducing a goal or activity, such as reaching for a specific toy, stacking big blocks, or turning something upside down and dropping it. You can hold your own toy or just pantomime holding one.

ALLERGIES AND INTOLERANCES

"Food intolerance" is a broad term that refers to any kind of unpleasant symptom that occurs after eating a specific food. These are sometimes also called "food sensitivities." Some reactions are minor, like a rash on the chin after eating strawberries. Other reactions can be more troublesome, like stomach pain, gas, and diarrhea after consuming milk. These reactions to milk are often caused by lactose intolerance and are common in older children but rare in babies.

A food allergy is a specific reaction triggered by your immune system. Your body reacts to a food as if it's a foreign invader, triggering an immune response. Some of these reactions can be serious and can lead to widespread symptoms like rashes and difficulty breathing. The most severe reaction, called anaphylaxis, is rare in young children. Most true food allergy reactions occur within minutes of eating a food.

It is not always easy to figure out if a symptom is caused by a food or what the food trigger might be. If you suspect your baby has a food intolerance or allergy, the best step is to keep a food log. Track what's being eaten and what kind of reaction happens next. Bring that record and your baby to your physician, and together you'll determine what's going on.

INTRODUCTION TO SPOON-FEEDING

Pediatricians used to believe that certain foods should be given to a baby in a certain order or avoided to prevent allergies. We now have excellent evidence that this is incorrect. Rather, it's *delaying* certain foods, or giving them too late, that increases allergy risk. The best way to feed your baby solids is to quickly offer a big variety. Here's a general guide:

Begin when your baby can hold their head up and seems interested. This typically occurs between four and six months.

Sit together as a family to share your meals. Your baby needs to be able to watch you eat to learn how to eat for themselves. Your baby should be able to see that you're giving them what you're eating. Avoid preparing separate, special, or different foods for your baby.

Commercial baby food is optional. Rather than buying baby food, feed your baby whatever you're eating, as long as you can mush it up so it's soft like a puree. Don't avoid rich flavors, like salt or garlic. A little bit of spiciness is fine, too. If it tastes good to you, it's good for your baby.

Mash up the food with a fork or small blender. Add a bit of water or milk to thin out the puree if needed.

Feed your baby a few spoonfuls and add words and facial expressions. Say things like, "That egg is good!" or "Mmmmm cheese grits." If your baby doesn't like it, say, "You didn't expect that, we'll try it another time."

Repeat once a day, at first. Once your baby is enjoying solids, move to feeding your baby solids two or three times a day.

SLEEP REVISITED

By four months of age, most babies are capable of sleeping through the night, at least for a stretch of six to eight hours. Some babies do this automatically. Others need a nudge. You and your partner can decide if it's time to sleep train, based on your child's temperament and your needs. If you'd like to get started, here are some steps to keep in mind:

Take advantage of the wake-eat-play cycle, in that order. Try not to feed your baby right before sleep time. You need to disconnect eating from sleeping, or your child may continue to want to eat in order to get back to sleep at night.

Try to put your baby down to sleep while they're still awake. If they fall asleep in your arms but wake to realize that you've left, they may decide they need you back.

Don't rush to pick them back up. When they wake up, or if they get upset when you put them down, don't pick them up. Be calm and reassuring, not apologetic. Be confident that your baby can do this.

Work with your partner to find a balance. Together, decide how much crying is okay. Every sleep training method involves tears (from babies and sometimes parents!). Quicker methods tend to involve more crying at first. Slower methods take more time but cause less crying. Crying won't hurt your baby, but it's reasonable to set time limits beforehand.

Be consistent. Studies on different styles of sleep training show that any method can work, as long as you're consistent and don't give up.

Dr. Knows Best: Don't Give Up on Sleep Training

Some babies are not easy sleepers. They won't fall asleep alone, won't nap, and won't stay asleep at night. Parents become exhausted and often give up sleep training efforts. But once you've started, you've already done some of the work. Keep at it! I know it seems like sleep training will never work. But it will *work if you stick to the plan. You, your partner, and your baby will all sleep better.*

HAVE FUN AND LEARN!

Being a dad can be exhausting. You've got to have fun, too. And fun and learning can happen together! Try out these fun activities as your baby grows from four to six months of age:

Sing. You don't have to know (or like) typical baby songs. Sing The Beatles, or Nirvana, or Lil Wayne. Maybe you can pull off Lady Gaga. Be careful with lyrics. You're going to hear your two-year-old singing them back to you soon.

Dance. Babies love rhythm, movement, and a funky beat. Your number one fan is in your arms. Shake your moneymaker!

Make faces. You're singing. You're dancing. It's time to get grooving. Your baby is ready to imitate your facial expressions. Start with a smile, but then move to frowns, pouts, wide-eyed stares, and anything else you can do with your face. Add funny noises to get some giggles.

Talk. You've been moving and communicating with expressions. Move on to verbal skills. Babies learn to talk by listening, copying, and paying attention to reactions. You don't need to talk like a Shakespearean actor. Just be yourself. Talk about what your baby is looking at or doing. Or watch football together and discuss why using the prevent defense with three minutes to go was a bad idea. Seriously, what was the coach thinking?

Go places. Your baby is ready to explore the world. Get out, take a walk or a drive, and keep talking and explaining. Introduce your baby to people, teach them how to order coffee, take them through a noisy car wash. Experience these things together, watch their cues, and encourage them to stay curious and keep exploring.

CHAPTER 3

7 TO 9 MONTHS

I call this age "personality plus." Your baby's own personality, their way of looking at the world, is in full bloom. It's now part of everything you do together. But there's more to think about than your baby's own built-in temperament. You need to keep your baby safe, guide them toward mastering certain skills, and help them grow into a better person. That's the "plus" part.

It's a challenge. You will need to adjust your approach and make accommodations for your child's likes, dislikes, strengths, and weaknesses. It can seem like a lot to tackle at first, but it can also be a lot of fun. You'll find this stage rewarding, exhilarating, and, at times, hilarious. Enjoy the ride together.

Throughout this chapter, you'll catch up on your baby's growth and development. You'll learn about a typical daily schedule and essentials for your baby, like feeding and nutrition, doctor's visits, new ways to play and bond, and different challenges to keep your baby safe and out of trouble. Your baby is ready. Let's go!

Your baby's temperament and interests affect their developmental trajectory. For instance, some babies are calm and contemplative. If a toy rolls away, they'll watch it go, and then play with something else. These babies are often slower in learning to creep or crawl because they don't have that strong need to get somewhere or get to something.

Other babies are go-getters. You can tell they want to be on the move. If a toy rolls away, they lunge after it, stretching, reaching, and wiggling to get to it. These babies tend to crawl sooner, pull up sooner, and sometimes develop motor skills before language skills. Of course, there are some babies in the middle.

Avoid comparisons. Milestones and expectations are okay as a guide, but every baby follows their own path. Not everything will happen when it's "supposed to," and it's not a competition. If you have concerns about your child's development, talk to your pediatrician.

Mental Development (Vision & Hearing)

By now, your baby should be able to see across a room clearly and distinguish colors. They will be able to move their eyes to track something moving quickly, like a rolling ball or a running sibling, and their hand-eye coordination is improving every day. Their eyes shouldn't cross and should always be moving in unison, or looking at the same thing.

Your baby will also start to respond to individual words, including—soon—their own names and power words like "No!" (They do not always listen, but they're beginning to understand.) Strange or unusual noises will get their attention quickly.

Physical Development (Movement & Growth)

Most seven-month-olds can roll both ways, front to back or back to front, and are starting to sit up by themselves without support. They can reach for an object and grab it cleanly with one hand in what's called a "raking grasp," which is using their whole hand and fingers as one unit rather than using individual fingers. An object can then be transferred back and forth between their hands. Babies at this age typically do not show any preference for either hand.

Growth by now has slowed a bit, to about two pounds of weight and an added quarter inch per month.

THE ROUTINE

Most (but not all) babies will sleep through the night by this age, which means you're packing more meals into the day. And naps are usually down to two or three times a day. Between seven and nine months, most babies take solid meals three times a day. The following example schedule accommodates these "usual" conditions, but it's fine to adjust. "Milk" here refers to nursing or taking a bottle. When possible, all solid meals should be eaten with one or both parents, together.

7 a.m.: Wake up, milk, then some playtime

8 a.m.: Breakfast, then more playtime

9 a.m.: First nap

11 a.m.: Wake up, milk, playtime

12 p.m.: Lunch, then more playtime

2 p.m.: Second nap

3 p.m.: Wake up, milk, playtime

5 p.m.: Dinner

6 p.m.: Bath, stories, singing (but not too much wild play)

7 p.m.: Bedtime, then parents get the evening to themselves

Dr. Knows Best: The Best Schedule

The best schedule for your family is what works for you and your baby. Think about when you or your partner works or attends classes and what times will be most practical for your family meals. Is your baby an early riser or a night owl? You may end up deciding that your baby's schedule works best shifted earlier or later. If that works, great!

CHECKUP SCHEDULE

Checkups at this age happen less frequently. After the six-month visit, your next scheduled doctor's visit will likely be at nine months of age. Your child's doctor will want to assess their physical growth as well as their motor, sensory, verbal, and social development. There may not be any vaccines needed at nine months, but your doctor will double-check to ensure your baby is protected. They'll also make sure your baby is moving toward independence by starting to feed themselves and falling asleep on their own. Don't forget your list of questions.

FEEDING & NUTRITION CHART

Seven to nine months is when babies transition to getting most of their nutrition from solid food. Some babies make this change sooner or later than others, and that's okay. Follow your baby's lead as their interest in food grows and as their interest in breast or bottle declines. There are some general rules of thumb, but don't try to force your baby to stay within these guidelines. If your mini-me is ready to forge ahead with more solids and less milk, that's fine; or, if they're tentative about solids, it's okay to go slower. Either way, eat as a family, set a good example, and continue to offer new foods.

MILK	WATER	SOLIDS
About 24 ounces of commercial formula or 4 or 5 nursing sessions per 24 hours	A few sips with every solid meal, best offered in a sippy cup	3 times a day, a mix of spoon-fed purees and a few other finger foods for practice

BABYPROOFING

Babies don't really anticipate danger or have any sort of common sense to stay out of trouble. So it's best to think about babyproofing early, *before* your baby is crawling and mobile. They will not (yet) learn from natural consequences or painful experiences. It's up to you to pro-tect them from things that can cause serious harm. Here are some tips for babyproofing now:

Lock up medicines and dangerous household items. All of these items (e.g., insecticides, oven cleaner, bleach, laundry detergents, firearms) should be well out of reach, ideally in a room the child can't enter. If you have any fire-arms, they should be locked up separate from ammunition.

Secure tall, heavy furniture. Any large furniture (e.g., bookcases, tall dressers, large televisions) needs to be attached to the wall. Babies will climb on them and will use the drawers of a dresser to make a sort of ladder.

Keep cords, including electric cords and lines from blinds, out of reach. They need to be tucked away behind heavy furniture or secured well above any possible reach of a child. Remember, babies will push toys over so they can climb up to dangerous things.

Stairs should be secured with gates. You'll need gates at the top and bottom. Don't depend on pressure gates for this. Use gates that screw securely into a solid wall or post.

Lock toilets and put away razors and toiletries. This is especially important in baby-accessible bathrooms.

Keep houseplants out of reach. Many are poisonous, and all have fascinating dirt that your child will love to spread around and taste.

SAFE TOYS

The best toys are ones that babies can touch and manipulate, with big, textured, chunky parts that are easy to grab, stack, and move. These toys will be chewed on and handled roughly, so look for sturdy, waterproof items that won't break or get soggy.

SAFE TOYS:

- Ball pits
- Large fidget cubes (smaller parts shouldn't break off)
- Stacking rings or blocks
- Shape sorters
- Toys for imaginary play (dolls, plastic food, etc.)
- Push-and-pull cars and trucks
- Heavy cardboard or plastic books

UNSAFE TOYS:

- Anything with a cord or string longer than seven inches
- Anything with a painted surface
- Small balls or marbles; if it can fit inside a toilet paper roll tube, it's too small
- Anything with parts or hinges that can pinch fingers
- Magnets or batteries that could possibly get loose
- Toy chests with closing lids
- Balloons
- Old toys made of unsafe materials

Communication is a crucial, emerging skill. You want to share your wisdom and experiences, and your baby loves your voice.

Set the scene. You and your baby need each other's attention. You can hold them on your lap, facing you, or sit across from them in their high chair. Either way, look each other in the eyes.

Talk about what's on your mind. It doesn't have to be anything especially important—no pressure.

Use your own normal speaking voice. Some people like to talk to babies in a high-pitched voice, and that's fine if you want to. Speaking a little slower than usual will help your baby keep up with the pace.

Don't dumb it down or use silly words. Speak the way you would to anyone, unless of course you're telling a silly story. In that case, make up any words you want.

Pause every once in a while, and let your baby speak. Wait until their turn is done before you speak again. They'll pick up on the back-and-forth of conversation, which helps them learn to not interrupt.

Feel free to add visual aids like finger puppets, a spoon, or a funny mask. Use your hands and your facial expressions, and add sound effects.

Repeat favorites. You may find a few stories, especially ones with acting or sound effects, that your baby especially loves.

CPR CERTIFICATION

It's a great idea for you and your partner to get certified in cardiopulmonary resuscitation (CPR). It's not difficult to learn, and if you're in a situation where it's necessary, you'll feel more confident and prepared. Visit the American Heart Association website to find an online or in-person class (CPR.Heart.org). Here's a brief refresher on the steps for simplified, hands-only CPR that can be performed by anyone. We'll start with the approach to an adult victim, followed by a few points to remember about children and infants. See page 106 for the steps to take with a choking infant or child.

For an adult victim:

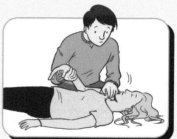

1. Make sure the scene is safe. Don't put yourself in danger to help a victim (for example, don't run into traffic).

2. Check if the victim is okay. If they're breathing or moving, call for help but don't start CPR.

3. Have someone call 911 and get an automated external defibrillator (AED) if one is nearby. As soon as it arrives, stop CPR and use the AED.

4. Push hard and fast in the center of the chest (these are "compressions").

5. Don't stop until trained help arrives.

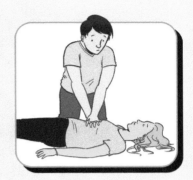

A few finer points can make CPR more likely to help:

→ Ideally, time the compressions to the song "Stayin' Alive," at 100 beats per minute.

→ Try not to lean on the victim during compressions. Let your hands come back up.

For a child or infant victim, there are just a few differences:

→ If you can, it's best to give rescue breaths in addition to the compressions of CPR, alternating two breaths with every 30 compressions.

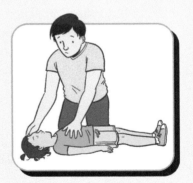

→ For a child, perform compressions using just the heel of one hand in the middle of the chest.

→ For an infant, perform compressions using two fingers pointing down in the middle of the chest.

NEW FOOD INTRODUCTION

Almost any food is appropriate at this age. Avoid foods that might be a choking hazard, like hard or raw vegetables, nuts, raisins, whole grapes, or tough meats. Avoid raw honey until 12 months of age (unpasteurized or "natural" honey can cause botulism in young babies). Otherwise, anything that's soft enough to squish easily between your finger and thumb is fair game.

It's best to have meals as a family. For example, you and your partner could trade off breakfast and lunch, and then both do dinner. To start a new food, begin by eating it yourself, and look for your baby's reaction. Chances are, they'll be watching you.

Say something like, "Oh, this is a mushroom omelet. It's good. Do you want some?" Then, offer a bit for your baby to taste. At six or eight months, they might need help getting a little piece to their mouth. Once they're reaching and grabbing, put a piece on their tray for them to handle. Feeling that texture is messy, but it's part of the learning and fun!

When your baby tastes something, they might make a face or gag if the taste or texture is new. Be positive and reassuring. Avoid saying, "Eww, that was yucky wasn't it?" and instead say something like, "What did you think of that? Yeah, it can be an acquired taste. Want some more?"

Follow your baby's lead, and don't force any foods on them. They'll soon learn to like what you're eating.

GOOD SOLID FOOD

Just about any food can be part of your little one's diet. The more variety, the better. You don't have to stick with traditional baby foods. A little salt, pepper, or garlic is fine, too. Bland and boring food is not required. Here are some ideas to get you started, but don't limit yourself! If your baby's not ready or eager to feed themselves yet, mash these up for spoon-feeding.

- **Well-cooked beans:** They contain iron and protein and are fun to eat pureed or individually by hand.
- **Soft-cooked vegetables:** Aim for the consistency of canned peas or carrots. Cook and cube sweet potatoes, carrots, squash—anything!
- **Canned veggies:** Pick low-salt varieties of green beans, mixed veggies, etc.
- **Scrambled eggs:** Soft enough for any age, scrambled eggs are a great source of iron and protein. Cook them up with cheese for more flavor.
- **Soft fruits:** Banana slices, cubed ripe peaches, or individual canned mandarin orange segments work great.
- **Cooked fruit:** Soften up cubes of apple or pear in the microwave, and let them cool.
- **Well-cooked soft pasta:** Grains like pasta and rice are vitamin fortified.
- **Crumbly meatballs or meat loaf:** Just like Grandma used to make!
- **Avocados:** These are tasty and easy to eat cubed or mashed. Squeeze on some lime.
- **Cereals:** Pick low-sugar, fortified cereals like Cheerios. Mash them in milk to start.

DEVELOPMENTAL GAMES

Your baby learns through play. At this age, they become more inquisitive and interactive and eager to spend time with you doing new things. Almost anything can become a game. Here are some ideas to get you started:

A Sunday drive. Put your baby in your lap, like they're in the driver's seat of a car, facing forward or backward. Hold their hands to the imaginary steering wheel, and take them for a "drive." There'll be bumpy roads (bounce!), fast roads (zoom!), uphills, downhills, stops. You get the picture. Vocalize what you see, making animal noises when you pass a farm and disco sounds when you drive by a nightclub.

Come and get me! Once your baby is starting to go places, whether scooting, rolling, or crawling, move a bit away so they can chase you. Say, "Oooo, baby gonna get me!" and give big hugs when they make it.

The nose game. Sit your baby in your lap. When they grab or touch your nose, make an appropriate nose sound like a honk, a beep, an "awoogah," whatever you like. Different parts of your face can make different noises.

Explore a drawer. Put your sock drawer on the floor, and let your baby paw through it and empty it out, and then fill it back up. You can do this with one of your kitchen cabinets (filled with pots or plastic tubs), a backpack with supplies, or anything that's safe and sturdy for your explorer to get their hands on.

Dr. Knows Best: Gagging Is Not Choking

Babies will sometimes gag when they taste new foods, which indicates surprise at the texture and taste. A gag is a funny look, sometimes with a red face and a brief pause in breathing. After a moment, a gagging baby will start making noises, and you'll know they're fine. The only treatment needed is reassurance. Stay calm. Don't grab your baby or make a scene. Gagging passes quickly. To avoid gagging, let babies feed themselves with their own hands.

CHOKING RESCUE

If your baby can cough or is making sounds, they are not choking. Let them cough it out. If a baby is truly choking, they will not be making any vocal sounds and will not be coughing or gagging. Only continue with the following choking rescue steps (previously called the Heimlich maneuver) if your child is truly choking.

If there is another adult present, have them call 911 while you begin the choking rescue steps.

1. Put your baby facedown across your forearm, with their head lower than their chest. Support their head with your palm, but don't twist their head or cover their mouth. You can brace your arm against your thigh for support.

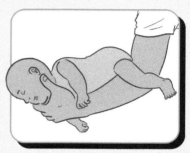

2. Use the heel of your other hand and give five sharp slaps to your baby's back.

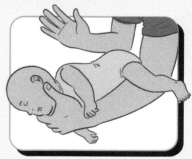

3. Turn them faceup, with their head remaining low. Using two or three fingers, push down in the middle of their chest, sharp and hard, five times.

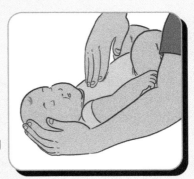

4. Repeat steps 1 to 3 until your baby starts to cry or cough.

5. If your baby loses consciousness (faints), call 911 immediately. Stop performing the choking steps, and start CPR (see page 100). Continue CPR until trained help arrives.

6. During CPR, if you feel comfortable giving rescue breaths, look in your baby's mouth before each set of breaths. If you can see anything blocking the airway, remove it. If you don't see anything, don't do blind sweeps with your finger or put anything in your child's mouth.

BABY MUSCLE EXERCISES

Your baby already does a lot of exercises on their own. Practicing standing, reaching for things while working on balance, and holding themselves up while you carry them on your hip are all great exercises that help with strength, motor control, and stability. Here are some ideas for more baby exercises. Keep these activities enjoyable. If your baby is getting tired or upset, it's time to stop and move on to another activity.

Sit on a big exercise ball. This is a great way to practice balance and work on core strength.

Reach and stretch. Move desired objects a little farther away, not to frustrate your baby, but to help them learn that stretching and grabbing at things can expand their world and reach.

"GetEmUps." Start with your baby on their back. Hold just their hands and help them use their abdominals to do a sit-up. Keep holding their hands, and help your baby get all the way from sitting to standing.

"Rollups," or "big swoops." Practice your baby rolling from back to front and front to back, giving some help at first, if needed. When they're good at it, mix things up by having them practice on an incline, in your lap, or on some other surface. Flip them back over with a big swoop noise so they laugh and want to try it again.

DECODING BABY TALK

Early vocalizations included grunts, squeals, raspberries, gurgles, and laughs. By now, your baby is probably starting to vocalize with the typical baby talk: babble. These are consonant-vowel pairs, often repeated, like "ma-ma," "ga-ga," and "da-da." At first, these noises have no specific meaning. Your baby is saying them for practice. When you respond to your child's baby talk, you assign meaning to their early babbles, and that's how your baby learns to speak. Here are a few tips to decode your baby's babbling:

- **Ba-ba:** This might be "ball" or "bottle." Or, less likely, "barbecue." Is your dog named Barney? It might be an early pronunciation.
- **Ga-ga:** My wife and I decided this noise from our son meant "hungry," and sure enough, within a few weeks he was using this noise to let us know he wanted to eat.
- **Ka:** I've met a few babies whose first word was "ka," as in "car." "Ka" can mean "leaving," "vehicle," or "taking a trip" all in one useful baby word.
- **Ma-ma:** There's only one likely meaning for this one. Cultures all over the world use double "M" words to mean "mother."
- **Da-da:** You know who you are. Own this babble the first time your kid says it. It's wonderful. It's you.

EXERCISE PARTNER

Your baby is getting stronger and faster, and you need to stay in shape to keep up! Here are some fun exercises for you, using your baby as a partner.

Hopalong: When babies stand, they often like to bounce up and down. Help them fly high in the air with a big lift and gently return to earth with every bounce.

Superman: Balance your baby belly-down on top of your head, and walk around your house saying "Superman" while doing squats or lunges. Beware of spit-up on this one!

Baby from space: Get down on your back and lift both knees straight up to the ceiling. Place your baby lying down with their chest right on your shins and their head and upper body past your knees. (The further forward your

baby, the more they'll have to use their own core strength to stay horizontal.) Bend your knees forward and back, and shift your legs left and right so your baby can fly. Make sound effects, too. Say, "Wooo wooo wooo, here comes the space baby!"

Baby bench press: This is another risky one for spitty babies, but you didn't become a dad to play it safe. Lie on your back on the floor or an exercise bench. Your baby is your weight. Lift

them straight up and then down, slowly, or to make it more challenging, shift them right and left. You could call them a baby bird, bat, dragonfly, or wrecking ball. Add appropriate noises and commentary.

TEETHING SYMPTOMS

You might think that teething hurts, but that's probably a myth. When it's been objectively studied, the most common symptom of teething is absolutely nothing. That's right. Most babies with teeth coming in experience no pain or symptoms whatsoever. Parents just notice, peeking in their mouth: Hey, a new tooth!

Some parents do seem to notice certain symptoms that cluster around tooth appearance. These symptoms are minor and have no significant impact on a child's health. If your child seems really ill, it is not teething. Consult their doctor.

The following symptoms can appear while babies are teething, though they may not be caused by teething:
- Increased fussiness
- Disrupted sleep
- Drooling
- Wanting to put things in their mouths
- A change in stools, like constipation, diarrhea, or an unusual color
- Rashes near the mouth
- Diaper rash
- An elevated temperature (A true fever, or measured temperature of over 100.4°F, is not caused by teething.)
- Cheek rubbing or ear pulling
- Cold symptoms like a runny nose or coughing

TEETHING

At about three or four months of gestation, long before birth, your baby's first teeth develop. That's right, 20 baby teeth were already completely formed when your child was born. They usually start to "erupt" around six or eight months after birth. (Erupting is the process of teeth moving toward the gum surface and then poking out.)

The first teeth to appear are usually the two central bottom ones, followed by their counterparts on top, but they don't always follow that order. On average, once teeth start to erupt, your baby will get one new tooth every month, though they may come in pairs every other month or otherwise kind of cluster together. Don't worry, none of these variations are due to a developmental problem, and none are a reflection of your baby's health. Teeth seem to come in when they feel like it.

For dental health, brushing should start when teeth erupt. Be gentle, and use a rice-size dot of fluoride-containing toothpaste twice a day.

If your baby seems uncomfortable while teething, you can offer something cold, massage their gums, try a teething toy, or use an occasional dose of oral acetaminophen. Do not use teething gels or tablets. Stay away from amber teething necklaces. These don't work and can strangle or choke your baby.

NAME RECOGNITION

Most babies start to recognize the sound of their own name at around seven months. They can't say it yet, but they know what it means. You can help your baby learn their own name (and yours!) with some simple steps.

1. **Say their name a lot.** Use their name from day one. If you've chosen a nickname, you can use that one instead. But try to use the same sound every time.

2. **Say it when you see them.** And when they see you. Say it to get their attention and when you want to tell them something.

3. **Reward them when they react.** This part is automatic: When your baby reacts to their name, I guarantee you'll smile.

4. **Turn their name into a song.** Or a rhyme, or a game. Let's say your son's name is Daniel. You can say, "Daaaaaaannnnn" until he looks at you, and then say "yul!" and pounce with a quick tickle.

5. **Use the name with different tones.** There's a "DANIEL!" of surprise: Where did you come from? A "Daniel!" of happiness: I caught you doing something cool. And a "Daaaniel" of alarm: Get your hands out of that flowerpot!

6. **Use your own name.** Or use your title, like "Dad" or "Daddy," and the names and titles of other people. This helps your baby learn the importance of each name and that different people have different names.

RELIABLE SLEEP ROUTINE

By now, many (but not all) babies sleep through the night. You may have achieved this already, either through good luck or a consistent sleep training routine, or a combination of both. If your baby isn't sleeping independently through the night, think about how much of a priority solid sleep is for you and your partner. You may decide to delay sleep training, or you can refer to page 117 for a variety of ways to teach your child independent sleep. When the time is right, you *can* do this!

Once independent sleep is established, it's best to stick with a consistent sleep schedule every single day. Start your bedtime routine at the same time, seven days a week, and go through all of the steps in the same order. Many families start with a bath, then reading, then perhaps prayers or snuggles. You might have a specific "go to sleep" song to end your routine (maybe "Baby Beluga," "Amazing Grace," or "Isn't She Lovely"). Then kiss your baby and leave them to fall asleep on their own.

There will be inevitable setbacks—maybe a rough night here or there. If your baby is sick, you'll probably indulge them with extra snuggles. But don't let these new habits erase the progress you've made. Stick to your sleep routine, and everyone will sleep better in the long run.

BABY SLEEP CYCLES

A baby's sleep architecture—the cyclical way their sleep is organized—is different from older children or adults. Understanding those differences can help you guide your baby to more consistent and restful sleep that's better for you *and* your baby. Here are the terms and concepts to know:

Length: The duration of a newborn's total daily sleep is between 10 and 18 hours per day. By seven or nine months, the range is narrower, from 9 to 12 hours of nighttime sleep, plus daytime naps. The science isn't clear on exactly why babies need more sleep than adults, but it seems important for brain and physical development.

REM sleep: REM sleep is when your eyes flicker around. It's the part of sleep when you have vivid, detailed dreams. Adults spend about a quarter of their sleep time in REM; your baby's REM time is probably closer to half. REM sleep helps consolidate and organize learning.

Cycle length: Adults experience sleep cycles of approximately one and a half to two hours, with "partial" awakenings at the end of some cycles. In infants, the cycles are shorter, about 45 minutes. Have you wondered why your baby seems to wake up 45 minutes after they fall asleep? It's when they come out of deep sleep and are easiest to arouse.

LEARNING INDEPENDENT SLEEP

Your baby wasn't born knowing how to fall asleep independently. They have to learn it. And like any other new skill for a baby, you can help them learn how to do it. There's no single best way—any of these methods can work, if used consistently. Refer back to Sleep Revisited on page 86 for some general sleep training guidelines. One of these options will work for you:

Ferberizing: Also known as "graduated extinction," starts with putting your baby down to sleep alone while they're still awake, after cuddle time or stories. Don't apologize. Be confident, and say, "Good night, sweetie. I'll see you tomorrow." Then leave the room. On the first night, if they cry after you leave, check on them every five minutes until they stop. Every night, increase the waiting time by one minute.

Cry it out: This is similar to Ferberizing, but you don't go in and check on your baby. You let them cry until they're done. This method works, and it's safe. But there are more tears, and it's not for everyone.

Camping out: This method is considered gentler. After you put your baby down, "camp out" by sitting in a chair in their room until they fall asleep. Don't hold or rock them, just be there. Every few nights, move that chair farther away from your baby's crib until you're in the hallway.

Wake and sleep: Rock or hold your baby until they fall asleep on you, then put them in their crib. Then deliberately wake them up, just a little, maybe with a rub of their feet. Try not to wake them all the way, just enough so they can fall asleep without you holding them.

Dr. Knows Best: Crying Won't Hurt Your Baby

Crying does not hurt your baby or cause unhealthy stress in any way. It's okay to allow your baby to cry at night while you're sleep training, as long as at other times, during the day, you're responsive to their cries. Don't let your baby's crying during a few weeks of sleep training worry you or make you stop training. Keep it up and keep it consistent.

READING TO BABY

Reading together is a wonderful way to get your baby to sleep, promote language skills, and have fun. At first, your baby might not have a long attention span, but it can become one of the best parts of your day. Reading together can be part of your sleep routine, and it's a good thing to do any time.

Set a good example. If your baby sees you reading, they'll want to get involved. Any reading material is good: books, magazines, newspapers, take-out menus. Save electronic books or tablets for older children.

Keep it short and simple. If your baby is bored (e.g., looking away, arching, or acting disinterested), take a break and try again later.

Sit your baby in your lap. That way, you can both see what you're reading.

Start with board books or cloth books. They can handle more wear and tear.

Pick books with color and simple words. Their eyes will be drawn to blocks of color and big letters.

Don't punish your baby or say something negative if they rip a page. It's part of exploring. Choose a sturdier book next time.

Add excitement. Use special voices for characters, sound effects, animal noises. It's all part of the fun!

Point and name things. Explain what they are or why they're there.

Repeat. Little ones love the same stories over and over, especially if you've nailed the voices and excitement of the story. Pretend you're on Broadway, performing nightly for your adoring audience.

SLEEPING MALFUNCTIONS

Was your baby sleeping well and has now regressed? Or perhaps they've never gotten the hang of a solid night's sleep. Whatever the cause of your baby's sleep malfunction, the best approach is to go back to your sleep training plan and stick with it. Here are several reasons for sleep issues:

They're not feeling well. Babies who are sick or coming down with a cold often have disrupted sleep.

They're feeling better. After a cold or illness, babies might need a refresher course on independent sleep patterns.

A change in routine. Almost anything that disrupts your baby's routine, such as vacations, visiting relatives, a parent traveling, or daylight savings time, can lead to sleep problems. Don't let a few nights of awakening become the new normal.

Sleep regressions. As babies grow and develop, they'll sometimes move two steps forward and one step back. Maybe your baby has learned to pull themselves up to stand in their crib but can't get back down.

Lack of independent sleep associations. If your baby hasn't learned to fall asleep independently, you will have night awakenings. Step back to square one to get on track, starting by allowing your baby to fall asleep alone.

FAMILY PHOTO ALBUM

Sharing a family photo album is a fun way to bond with your baby and practice book-holding skills. Tell your baby about your family (including silly tales and secrets!) and have them learn the faces of people in their life.

Use a big album that can get sticky. Babies at this age aren't gentle. They like to grab, and you shouldn't discourage them. You may want to print extra-big photos and create a waterproof, easy-to-clean album.

Have your baby sit in your lap and turn the pages with you. This is a great way to practice reading and motor skills.

Include your family photos and those of your partner. Start with people they've met and places they've seen, but expand to more-distant relatives, friends, and unique places.

Talk about the photos. Who's in the picture? What's happening? Where were they? Why do they look happy?

Point as you go, and help your baby point. Soon, you'll be able to ask your baby to point for you by prompting, "Where's Grandma? Where's the birthday cake?"

Imitate sounds and voices. Yes, even your mother-in-law's. You'll sound great, and your partner will love it.

Tell your baby family stories. Shared stories and experiences are one of the things that make you a family. You'll end up repeating them, and sometimes embellishing them, and that's okay.

SETTING UP A SAFE ZONE FOR MOVEMENT: PULLING UP, CLIMBING, AND EXPLORING

Soon, your baby will be moving. At first, they may be scooting or rolling, but before long, they'll be crawling. At this age, babies don't have a sense of danger or the ability to stay out of harm's way. You need to be your baby's first line of defense by creating a "safe zone," or giant safe area, in your home. That way, you can stay in the safe zone with them and not have to watch their every move. You might make the living room or a family room the safe zone. Wherever you create this, make sure it's physically blocked off with doors, furniture, or baby gates. Then look for the following things in the zone, and fix or remove them:

Sharp corners on furniture. Cover these with pads, or remove the furniture altogether.

Fireplaces. Cover corners with pads, and if possible close these up entirely. Besides the burn risks when in use, they're a sooty mess.

Furniture that can tip over.
Remove or attach furniture to
the wall so nothing topples on
your baby.

Drawers or cabinets. Secure
each drawer and cabinet that
might pinch a finger or be used
as a ladder.

**Electric cords or cords
from blinds.** These must
be affixed high up or tucked
securely behind furniture. Or
remove them.

**Houseplants, pet feeding
dishes, or small decorative
items.** Remove these, as all will
end up in your baby's mouth.

Any precious household item. Remove, because your
baby *will* find it.

Televisions. Keep these unavailable to your baby. It's best
not get your baby too involved with electronics and screen
entertainment just yet.

CRAWLING ASSISTANCE

Most babies start to crawl between seven and ten months of age, though many won't start until later. And some will skip traditional crawling, instead getting around with a scoot, roll, or "commando crawl" until they start walking. Late crawling is not usually anything to worry about, but if you'd like to nudge crawling skills along, here are some things to do:

Tummy time. Start early, and make sure there is plenty of it (page 56).

Mirror play. This encourages your baby to reach out and stretch toward that baby in the mirror.

Practice rocking on hands and knees. You may have to help them get into this position, then you can gently help them rock. Sing a song to add rhythm.

Place toys a little out of reach. Don't tease or be mean about this, but let your baby strive to reach for things sometimes. You shouldn't always make things easy.

Decrease your use of strollers, swings, bouncers, or saucers. Providing this kind of support doesn't help your baby develop independence. They're fine for occasional use, but give your baby time to get around on their own.

Don't use "walkers." These are unsafe and slow motor development.

Get down and crawl with your baby. They will try to keep up!

Provide just a little support. Hold up their torso while they're in a crawling position. But don't do all the work yourself.

Try frequent, short practice sessions. These are better than occasional, longer attempts for little attention spans.

Dr. Knows Best: Enjoy the Mess

Babies love to explore and experience the world through all of their senses. That includes touching, grasping, manipulating, and sometimes breaking things. They need to feel and squeeze things like finger paint, scrambled eggs, shaving cream, and vanilla pudding. Things are going to get messy, and that's okay. You will never look back on your life and wish you were cleaner or more organized.

FIRST AIRPLANE TRIP

Between seven and nine months is usually a good time to travel. Your baby likes to meet new people and experience new things. But it's not always easy! There are ways to make your baby's first airplane trip more successful, or at least reduce the risk of a disaster. Whatever you do, you'll need flexibility, a sense of humor, and ideally a partner to share the extra work.

Pick a good time for your flight. You know your baby and when they're more likely to be in a good mood. Keep in mind that flights earlier in the day are less likely to be delayed.

Look into ways to bypass the security line. Families with young children might be able to skip ahead, depending on the airport and tickets.

Consider buying them a seat. You may be able to hold your young baby on your lap, but that gets uncomfortable and limits room, especially on a longer flight. The extra expense of a separate seat where you can strap them into their car seat may be worth it.

Leave your big stroller behind or check it. That big fancy thing with all the gizmos is a nightmare to get around an airport and onto a plane. Use a cheap, small, light umbrella-style stroller for trips.

Carry on essentials like food, formula, diapers, wipes, plastic bags, and extra clothes. Flights get delayed, so bring extras.

Bring toys. Take a few favorites and a few new ones to keep baby busy during the flight.

CHANGING DIAPERS IN CLOSE QUARTERS

Stuck on a plane or in a small public bathroom? Here are a few tricks and tips:

Do a diaper change before the flight. No matter how bad the bathroom is in the airport, it's better than the one on the airplane.

Use an overnight diaper for the trip. Overnight diapers are bulkier and hold more urine. You still need to change a poopy diaper, but an overnight diaper can buy you a few hours if they're just wet.

Keep outfits simple. The best ones are those that can easily snap all the way off and don't have fussy layers.

Ask a flight attendant for help. Have them find you the best changing area. Some lavatories have changing tables, or you can use the top of the toilet lid or the floor of the galley area in a pinch.

Be prepared with a mini diaper bag. You'll need two diapers, wipes, two disposable bags, and maybe a small tube of cream in a sealable plastic bag. There won't be room for your whole diaper bag in a small airplane bathroom.

Take off clothes at your seat. Your baby's clothes, I mean.

Dispose mindfully. Double-bag soiled diapers before disposing them. If you forgot bags, ask the flight attendant for some.

REPEAT SOUNDS

Sounds are a rich part of your baby's world. Loud or unexpected sounds can be scary, like a vacuum cleaner or a flushing public toilet. Certain sounds have a specific meaning, like a dog's bark or an "Uh-oh!" Other sounds might mean Mom or Dad is on the phone or it's time for dinner. And some sounds are just fun to listen and relax to. Use these ideas to help your baby learn to enjoy and use the great variety of sounds by imitating and repeating them.

→ Say words a little slower, and repeat them. Especially words to label what your baby is doing or looking at.

→ Repeat and explain your baby's words. If they say, "Dada," you can point and indicate yourself. "That's right, here is Dada."

→ Don't limit yourself to words as vocalizations. Noises that mean things include "yum," "mmmmmmmm," or a gasp of surprise.

→ Imitate and explain other noises in your world. It's all good: everything from a cat's meow to the noise when the toaster is done. "Ding! That means it's time for toast!"

→ For scary noises, warn your baby in advance. Make it a silly game. "You know what's coming? It's the vacuum cleaner! It's going to be loud! Get ready for VRRRROOOOM!"

→ Explain surprise noises, especially ones that make you jump. "Woo woo woo, that's an ambulance siren!"

INTRODUCING FIRST WORDS

The way to encourage your baby to speak and learn words is for you to use them. Use words to label and explain things throughout the day. Start by talking about what your baby is looking at or touching, what time of day it is, or what you're doing. This will come naturally if you stay in the habit of talking with your baby.

Most early words are nouns: people, places, and things. Make sure to use consistent labels for the people in your baby's life. You, your partner, and grandparents traditionally use titles rather than given names (e.g., "Daddy," "Papa," and "Grandma"). You'll also call yourself these things in the third person, at least at first, as in "Daddy is going to work now."

The other people in your home can be called whatever sounds natural, like "Claire," "Sister," or "Aunt Brenda." You'll want to use names for your pets, too, especially cats and dogs. Babies love to point at and name pets.

You should also name places you go: "school," "church," "grocery store," and "coffee shop" are all good early words. You'll use phrases to explain how you're getting there, like "Let's go in the car" or "Time for a walk."

Routine parts of the day need labels, too, like "breakfast," "nap," and "bath time." You'll want to label your baby's favorite toys, like "ball," or give a specific name for a favorite stuffed animal, like "Ducky." Favorite foods and common objects could include "banana," "cup," "phone," and "cookie."

SENSORY GAMES

Sensory games and activities help your baby coordinate and organize their senses, especially touch, so they can explore the world with confidence and creativity. These activities are often messy and always fun! Here are a few ideas to get you started:

Baby-safe finger paints. You can make "paint" out of instant vanilla pudding. Or mix 2 cups of corn starch into 1 cup of cold water, then slowly add 4 cups of very hot water, stirring as you add, until you have a custard-like paste. Add food coloring to either one. Let the mixture cool, then squeeze, rub, and play!

Water play. The tub is fun, but filling a shallow tray (like a cookie pan) with water and adding a few water-safe toys is equally splashy. It's safer, too, for semi-supervised play. Try sponges, things that float, and things that sink.

Bubbles. Try blowing bubbles at your baby. Make a game out of touching and grabbing the floating bubbles.

Rice play. Grab a tray or box and fill it with raw white rice and some toys. Encourage your baby to pour and scoop for fun, with less mess than a sand table.

Cloud dough. Mix about a cup of baby rice cereal (that dry stuff that tastes like the cardboard box it comes in) with a few tablespoons of warmed coconut oil. Once it cools, you'll get a moldable, clumpy, doughlike substance that's a whole lot of fun to scoop around in your hands. (Thanks to Dayna Abraham's blog, LemonLimeAdventures.com for this great idea!)

Dr. Knows Best: Take a Break

This book contains a lot of ideas for keeping busy with your baby, like how to have fun together and how to help your baby learn new things. But don't feel that you need to be "on the job" all the time. You do not have to fill your baby's every moment with developmental games and learning opportunities. Make time for relaxing and just hanging out, too. You deserve a break.

BABY SIGN LANGUAGE

You and your baby have been learning to communicate using sounds, gestures, and facial expressions. Some families like to use baby sign language, or specific hand motions with meanings. Many look like common-sense pantomimes of what they mean, so they're easy to remember.

If you get into the habit of using these as you speak, your baby will use the same signs to communicate by eight or ten months. Repeat them frequently, but don't drill your baby. Use them as they come up in everyday interactions. Here are some common early signs and one advanced sign for those of you who want to get ahead:

HUNGRY

1. Cup your hand around your neck.
2. Then move your hand down to your stomach.

MORE

1. Pinch your thumbs and fingers together on both hands to make the letter "O."
2. Then touch them together in front of you.

DRINK

1. Make a cup shape with your hand.
2. Then bring it up to your mouth.

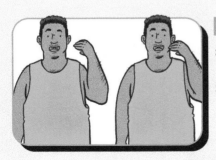

FOOD (OR "EAT")

1. Pinch your fingers against your thumb.
2. Then bring your hand to your mouth.

ALL DONE

1. Hold up your hands with your palms facing you.
2. Then turn them both forward.

THANK YOU (ALSO "YOU'RE WELCOME" IN REPLY)

1. Touch your straightened fingers to your chin.
2. Then bring your hand forward.

ELEPHANT (ADVANCED)

1. Start with your hand near your nose.
2. Move it down and out in the shape of an elephant's trunk.

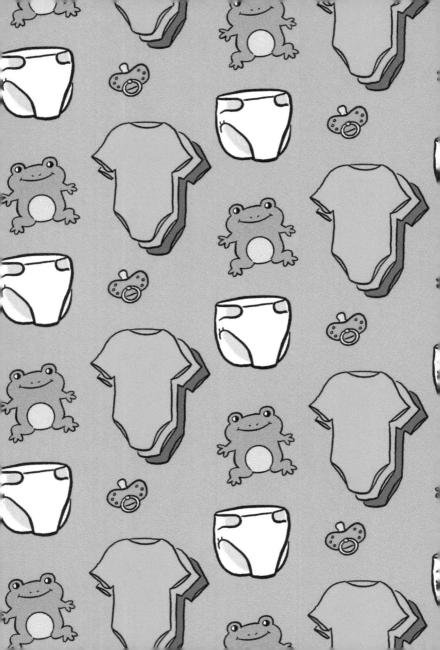

CHAPTER 4

10 TO 12 MONTHS

Babies at this age are busy little explorers and scientists, eager to figure out how the world works. Your baby will enjoy more complicated toys and activities, as well as interactions with new people, places, and things. What you think of as commonplace, your baby will find fascinating or hilarious. You must be there to guide them and keep them safe, but you shouldn't insist they do things your way or always do what you want to do. Let their independence blossom.

Remember that your partner needs you, too. Don't neglect this part of your life. There have been a lot of changes, both physical and mental. By now, the fog of exhaustion should be lifting. Spend time with your partner, and make time for your own hobbies and interests. It's not all about the baby.

This chapter starts with an overview of changes and development in your 10- to 12-month-old. Then it moves on to an example routine and a simple guide to food, nutrition, and doctor visits. After that, it explores more step-by-step expert "dad guides" and tasks to help you and your baby grow together.

GROWTH AND DEVELOPMENT

Your baby is becoming a toddler. This term is traditionally used around 12 months, since that's when many babies take their first unsteady steps.

At this age, there's even more variability in what's considered normal growth and development. Your baby may be chugging along in some areas, but behind in others. What's most important is their overall trajectory. Your baby should be progressing in these developmental areas:

→ **Gross motor skills:** big muscle stuff, like crawling and pulling up

→ **Fine motor skills:** using their hands

→ **Social development:** interacting with other people

→ **Problem-solving:** figuring out how things work

→ **Language:** both expressive and receptive

Typically, pediatricians won't worry too much if a child is behind in one area, but if your child is falling behind in several ways, discuss this with their doctor.

Mental Development (Vision & Hearing)

At this age, your baby should be able to see very well, focusing on both near and far objects, and tracking fast motion. Vision is also becoming integrated with motor control, so your child can spot an object, pick it up, and manipulate it.

Hearing and listening skills should be improving, too. Your baby probably knows some common words like "ball," "bottle," or "snack." A "No!" might not stop their exploration entirely, but they'll probably pause and look up at you to make sure you really mean it.

Physical Development (Movement & Growth)

Babies at 10 months old can travel to where they want to go, often by crawling. They can usually pull up from sitting to standing, and they'll soon be cruising around while holding onto furniture or your hands.

The average growth at this age is about 13 ounces and about a half inch of height per month. By 12 months, babies will have about tripled their birth weight and increased their height by 50 percent, though this varies and is affected by their parents' sizes, among other factors. At 12 months, your baby's brain is about 60 percent the size of an adult's. That's why their heads look big!

THE ROUTINE

Most babies at this age take two naps, totaling between two and two and a half hours of sleep, plus 11 or 12 hours of sleep at night, hopefully all in one stretch! Your baby may be trying to shake off taking naps, but it's usually best to maintain two naps a day until 15 months or so.

Offer your baby food—similar to what you're eating—at breakfast, lunch, and dinner, plus one or two snacks. Liquid meals (nursing or a bottle) should have started to dwindle down to about three or four times a day. Here's a sample schedule:

7 a.m.: Wake up, milk, then playtime

9 a.m.: Breakfast

10 a.m.: Nap, then milk or snack

12 p.m.: Lunch

2 p.m.: Milk

3 p.m.: Nap

5 p.m.: Dinner, then bath

7 p.m.: Last milk, then bedtime

Dr. Knows Best: Encourage Independence

Your baby is striving to learn new skills and do things for themselves. For the first time, you may have to step back and let them make their own decisions. Sometimes they won't do things "properly" or "efficiently," and you'll need to let them figure it out. Let your baby choose which shirt to wear and let them grab toys or food, even if it makes a mess.

There's just one checkup scheduled here: the one-year visit! It's a "happy birthday" visit, and your child's unofficial graduation from baby to toddler. At the one-year checkup, your baby's pediatrician or family doctor reviews their growth and development and performs a careful exam.

At this age, your baby is becoming more aware of their surroundings and might be frightened of the doctor and office. Stay calm and reassuring. Your doctor knows how to smooth things over. There will also be essential recommended vaccines. Stay up-to-date to ensure that your baby is safe and protected.

FEEDING & NUTRITION CHART

By this age, your baby should be eating the same foods you eat and typically at the same mealtimes—breakfast, lunch, dinner, and one or two snacks. Avoid any junk that's commonly called "snack food," including chips, puffs, and other low-nutrition packaged foods. Water should be offered in a sippy cup at meals. The following are general guidelines for daily intake, though in practice, don't count calories or measure portions. Expect meals to be a bit erratic, with one huge meal followed by a few picky or smaller ones. That's what kids do.

GRAINS	FRUITS & VEGETABLES	DAIRY	PROTEIN
5 servings (¼ to ½ slice bread or ¼ to ½ cup whole grain cereal, rice, or pasta)	5 servings (¼ cup each)	3 servings (½ cup milk or ¼ cup yogurt or cottage cheese or 1 ounce cheese)	2 servings (1 ounce meat or ½ egg or 1 tablespoon peanut butter or ¼ cup beans or lentils)

BABYSITTER SEARCH

You may be lucky enough to have relatives who will look after your baby. But sometimes you'll need a paid sitter. Here are some tips on finding and vetting a good one:

Think about what you need and what you feel comfortable with. Do you have twins, a small premature baby, or a child with special health care needs? You might need to go pro. But for most babies, a trusted adult or older teen is fine.

Start with personal recommendations. Look to neighbors, friends, teachers, and the people you trust. They may have good leads on sitters nearby.

Check local bulletin boards. Local community centers, churches, or schools may have a board with sitter recommendations. Or check out virtual boards online.

Research the sitter's experience. Ask for a list of references or experience. Babysitting or experience raising younger siblings counts. CPR training or a formal babysitting class is a plus, especially for younger sitters.

Check references. Don't just look at the list.

Test them out firsthand. After a short meet and greet interview, you might want to hire the candidate. But consider trying them out first, staying home that first night to see how things go.

Ask your child. I know your baby's not talking yet, but they can still "tell" you if they like the new sitter. If they're happy, playing, and interacting, that tells you something. If your baby and sitter don't hit it off, maybe look for someone else.

STRANGER ANXIETY

Fearfulness around strangers is a normal developmental step that often begins around eight months. Some babies prefer familiar adults and become fussy, tearful, or withdrawn at new faces. Seeing someone new may also make them afraid that you're leaving. Here are some tips that can help:

Don't dismiss or ignore the anxiety. Be kind and ease your baby through these experiences.

Make it easier. Introduce strangers in a safe space, like your home.

Use playtime. Let a new friend play with you and your baby together at first.

Let your baby hold your hand, sit in your lap, or hug a lovey.

Stay calm. Try not to get tense, loud, or excited.

Be patient. You can't push your child into this.

Stay close. Especially at first, stay nearby and don't sneak away.

Reassure the stranger. Let Aunt Janet take it slow, too, waiting before picking up your child.

Try frequent, short exposures. If you have an anxious child, don't avoid strangers. That reinforces the worry. Instead, have daily short exposures.

GET OUT!

Your baby loves to visit new places and meet new people, even if it's a little scary at first. The best way to encourage your baby is to make frequent, short excursions. Don't feel like you need to go to places that are expensive or that only cater to children. Any place that has people and activity can be exciting and fun. Here are some ideas to get started:

→ **Supermarket:** Stroll around, say "hi" to people, and check out the colorful produce or floral department.

→ **Bowling alley:** It's noisy and full of exciting things to look at.

→ **Small local park:** Bring a picnic blanket, but don't expect your child to stay put.

→ **Construction site:** Huge machines can be fun to look at from a distance. You'll likely be able to get closer at smaller neighborhood sites.

→ **Craft store:** There are lots of things to see and touch. Wash your child's hands first, and again after the visit.

→ **Outdoor farmers' market or art show:** There will be plenty of people and things to look at and talk about.

→ **Dog park:** Watch, talk about, and point at the dogs from outside the fence.

→ **Pet store/animal shelter:** The danger here is that you'll leave with a bigger family.

→ **Your partner's office (or your office):** Your baby will be the center of attention!

THE FIRST HAIRCUT

Some babies are born with thick hair that just keeps growing; others are born almost bald or become bald as their hair falls out. Is it time for that first haircut? You're getting close if your baby's hair keeps falling in their eyes or is getting on their nerves, or if you and your partner think the time is right.

You can certainly go to a family barber or salon, but why not do that first haircut on your own? No matter how it turns out, you'll have a story to tell and some photos to share. And you can always go to the barber afterward.

You'll need:

→ **A well-rested, clean, and calm baby.** Don't attempt this if your child is strung out, upset, or covered with sticky food.

→ **A chair.** It's best if it's high, or your baby can sit in your partner's lap.

→ **A comb, brush, and spray bottle of water.**

→ **Towels.** These double as capes.

→ **Barber shears/scissors.** These are sharp and cut hair much better than household scissors.

→ **Optional: electric trimmer.** Maybe skip this if you don't have experience.

Tips:

→ Distract your child with a movie or new toy.

→ Wet their hair first.

→ Cut small snips; don't try to take all the hair off at once. In fact, you don't even have to complete the job in one day. Pause if your baby needs a break.

→ Keep your hand between the shears and your baby's scalp.

PACIFIER WEANING

Is it time get rid of the pacifier? There's no one way that always works without resistance, but here are some ideas that might make things easier. Whatever you do, don't give your child a hard time. Be calm and reassuring.

Cold turkey: This isn't for everyone, but you can discard all of the pacifiers so there is no temptation. Sometimes, this method works very well, and quickly, too. If your baby is very upset, it's best to back off and come up with another approach.

Replacement: This is often used along with one of these other methods. Get a new lovey or stuffed animal for your child to hold.

Set limits: Declare that binky is only for in the crib (or in the car). Say it like you mean it and enforce the rule at all times. It can be helpful to let your child throw the pacifier across the room and say "bye" when you take them out of their crib in the morning.

Gradual wean: Start by declaring a few hours in the day as "no-pacifier" time, and then gradually build up that time every few days. Keep the pacifier out of sight when it's not allowed, and don't be in a rush to give it back when the time ends.

WHEN TO LET GO OF THE PACIFIER: WHAT THE EXPERTS SAY

Letting go of the pacifier can be difficult. When do you really need to stop? Here's what the experts say:

- The American Academy of Pediatric Dentistry (AAPD) recommends that children stop what's called "non-nutritive sucking" (sucking on pacifiers, thumbs, etc.) by age three.
- The American Dental Association (ADA) calls for children to stop pacifier use by age two.
- The American Academy of Pediatrics (AAP) encourages pacifier use in young babies less than six months old because it can reduce the risk of sudden infant death syndrome (SIDS). However, they encourage discontinuation between six and 12 months because of an increased risk of ear infections.
- Several breastfeeding advocacy organizations, including La Leche League International, discourage all but very limited pacifier use for short periods of time at any age.

The bottom line: There is no clear consensus and no strong evidence of an age when pacifier use must be discontinued. Weaning later may contribute to dental issues or ear infections, but you have to weigh that against your child's attachment and the soothing reassurance they've come to rely on.

Whatever you decide, keep this in perspective. Your baby isn't smoking or drinking or doing anything terribly harmful. They will give up their pacifier on their own eventually.

NEUTRALIZE A RUNNER

Do you have a runner on your hands? Some kids will take any chance to dash off across a parking lot or store. They're too young to learn what's dangerous, and they can be really fast and difficult to catch! They're running because they love freedom and exploring, not to be naughty, bad, or disrespectful. Here are some steps to keep a runner out of trouble:

1. **Safety first.** If your child is an aspiring Olympic sprinter, you must ensure their safety by keeping a hand on them when you're somewhere dangerous, like a parking lot. Don't unstrap your runner from the car seat until you're ready to give them your complete attention.

2. **Wait.** Developmentally, your child will be able to learn restraint soon and will respond to your calls. But they can't do it yet, so you may just need to stay in enclosed places to keep them safe. This does not last forever.

3. **Practice "Freeze!"** Parents say "stop" a lot to kids, and that word means too many different things to remain effective. Save "Freeze!" for when you need your child to stop running. Practice it like a game, with rewards and fun, and let your child "freeze" you, too.

4. **Go!** Go to places where your young Flo-Jo or Usain Bolt can really let 'er rip. A grassy park is ideal. A tired toddler can't keep running as fast.

Dr. Knows Best: All Discipline Requires Love

You're going to use several different strategies or tools to teach your child to behave. All of them rely on the same essential foundation: love. Your baby has to feel loved and appreciated for exactly who they are, even when they make mistakes. This creates confidence and security, so they're willing to take risks and learn from their experiences. For every correction or instruction, there should be 10 times as many hugs and smiles.

DISCIPLINE

The word discipline means "to teach," as in teaching your child to behave. Good behavior isn't automatic; it has to be taught and learned. Teach your child discipline using these tactics:

Modeling: This is crucial at every age. You need to behave the way you want your child to behave. That includes taking turns, being a good sport, and being respectful of others. Your child watches and copies everything you're doing.

Attention: You have to be there, mentally and physically, paying attention and giving feedback. Notice when your child does something right. Show them when you're proud.

Ignoring: Undesirable behavior should often be ignored (as long as it's not dangerous). You don't always have to respond. In fact, responding to unwanted behaviors sometimes makes young children want to do them more.

Positive reinforcement: That means a reward *after* your child does the right thing. A reward doesn't have to be a tangible item; a sincere "thanks" and a smile is often the best reward, especially when accompanied by a specific positive comment like "Great job cleaning up!" Mix that up with an occasional tangible reward, too, like a trip for ice cream or a small new toy.

Punishment: This should be your last resort. At this age, I think it's only appropriate as a response to aggressive behavior like hitting. Punishments should be very brief, like a short time-out, and should be followed immediately with the return of love and affection.

DEFUSING TANTRUMS

Tantrums often start around 12 months of age, sometimes earlier. They're an expected, normal part of development. Babies know exactly what they want but lack the patience to wait and the ability to communicate their frustration in words. Here are some steps to help make it through:

1. **Avoid them if you can.** Some situations bring out the worst in your child. Skip situations that you know will result in a tantrum if you can.

2. **Try a distraction during the lead-in.** In the moments leading up to a tantrum, you should not "give in." Do not give your child what they're whining about. If you do, they'll quickly learn that a tantrum is the best way to get what they want. Instead, turn the situation around by distracting them or doing something silly and unexpected.

3. **During the tantrum, stay safe, calm, and close.** When your baby is really upset, don't abandon them; keep them safe and stay close. But don't give them hugs or reassurance, and don't reward their behavior. Make sure they're safe and wait it out without talking or offering to help.

4. **After the tantrum, all your love can return.** Hold them and hug them. Remember that tantrums aren't to spite you or get back at you; they're not about you at all.

BABY'S FIRST FIRST-AID KIT

You don't need an extensive list of first-aid supplies, but stocking a few essential items for an unexpected injury or illness can save time and hassle. Here's a checklist of what to keep handy:

- **Contact information for your sitter, pediatrician, and pharmacy.** Include your own contact info on the card. Keep it handy if you need to do a sudden drop-off.
- **A baby thermometer.** An inexpensive digital thermometer is best. Get something that is small, light, and fairly unbreakable.
- **Saline nasal drops.** This is the single best treatment for babies with stuffy noses.
- **Bulb syringe or other nasal suction device.** Use this after the saline drops to decongest a stuffy nose.
- **Acetaminophen (brand name Tylenol or any generic).** Check with your baby's doctor for the correct dose of the version that you've purchased. The products labeled for infants include a handy syringe to make dosing easier. Write the correct dosage on the box with a big black marker. Those boxes are hard to read, and doses for younger babies aren't always on the package.
- **Bandages and antibiotic ointment.** The best, most important first aid after a cut, scrape, or burn is to clean the injury with cool, running water. Putting on a dressing with antibiotic ointment afterward is a good idea, but be sure your baby can't rip the bandage off and put it in their mouth.

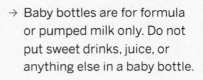

DENTAL HYGIENE

Good dental hygiene helps keep teeth healthy and establishes routines and expectations for years to come. Here are some quick tips to keep in mind:

→ Baby bottles are for formula or pumped milk only. Do not put sweet drinks, juice, or anything else in a baby bottle.

→ Don't put your baby to bed with a bottle of anything (see illustration).

→ Aim to stop using a baby bottle entirely around 12 months of age.

→ If you use a pacifier, don't dip it in sweet things; just keep it clean. Wash or run it through the dishwasher when needed.

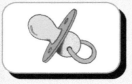

→ Start brushing your baby's teeth twice a day as soon as the first tooth appears.

→ Use a soft, child-size tooth-brush. Be gentle. The goal here isn't perfection but to establish a positive lifelong habit. Back off if your baby is upset. The total brushing time should be brief, just a few seconds per tooth.

→ Alternatively, use a soft "finger toothbrush" at first.

→ Use a small, rice-size dab of fluoride-containing toothpaste. Don't expect young babies to spit after brushing—that's okay.

→ Brushing teeth should be a last step before bedtime. Don't offer milk or food afterward.

→ Start flossing when your baby has two teeth that touch. Again, the goal isn't perfection here, you just want to start a habit that your baby will grow into. Plastic disposable flossers make this easier.

SEPARATION ANXIETY

For many babies, separation anxiety begins around nine months as they learn object permanence. This is a normal developmental step when babies realize that things still exist, even when they can't see them.

Separation anxiety can vary widely. Some babies feel this much stronger and for longer. The same baby will sometimes react more strongly, perhaps because they're already hungry or tired. Though you might not be able to completely avoid tearful separations, there are ways to make them easier.

Make separations short and sweet. Say, "Bye! I'll be back soon!" Give them a kiss, and then take off.

Be consistent. Have a routine that leads up to a drop-off, so your child learns what to expect.

Include warnings, though not too many. Say, "Five minutes until school" or "We're passing through the gate; drop-off soon." On the other hand, too many warnings make drop-off sound serious. Your warnings should be matter-of-fact and not apologetic.

Practice. This is key. More frequent, brief separations starting early pave the way for success.

Don't add to the negative emotion. If your baby is getting upset, don't make sad faces and pout along with them. Your message should be positive and short.

You've probably already been copying your baby's movements (see page 83), but have you tried using a mirror? Mirrors are great developmental toys. Your baby can practice postural control, their own facial expressions, and unique dance moves. You can even add an extra layer of movement and silliness by joining the fun!

1. **Find a solid, floor-length mirror.** Your baby will slap and push on it, so make sure it's solid and bolted to the wall.

2. **Sit behind your baby.** Peek around them and see yourself in the mirror. Your baby should be facing the mirror so they're mostly looking at themselves.

3. **Hold their hands.** Move them around like a marionette.

4. **Dress them (or yourself!) up.** Big silly hats or gloves are great. Mix it up.

5. **Tell short stories.** Add movements, both small and large. "There's a cat up in a tree, let's pet it," or "Let's fly to the moon!"

6. **Don't leave out the sound effects.** "I hear a lion roaring! We'd better run. Wait! I think he has a thorn in his paw, let's pull it out."

7. **Add games.** Try throwing soft things at the mirror or playing hiding games by putting a toy under a blanket.

8. **Turn it around.** After your baby gets good at mirror play, have them hold *your* hands and move them around. This encourages independence and two-way interactions, and it's a fun opportunity for silliness.

SLEEP TRAINING

By now, your baby *can* sleep on their own, all through the night. But that doesn't mean they'll do it automatically. It's a learned skill, and some babies make this easier than others. It's never too late to start a plan for everyone—baby and parents—to get a good night's sleep.

→ Create a consistent bedtime routine. Keep it calm, with reading or lullabies after a bath.

→ Continue consistent sleep training. Do it at a time when you're at home. Don't do it when you're on vacation, when your child is sick, or when the grandparents are visiting.

→ Make sure your child has their own comfortable, cool, quiet, dark sleep space. You may need to move them to their own room if you haven't already.

→ Choose a sleep training method and stick with it. Any technique will work if you follow the plan. Revisit some common sleep training techniques on page 117.

Don't give up. Your baby may be upset at first, and there will be tears. This will not last long and will not hurt your baby. It is worth it to get better sleep, and you and your baby will be much happier when you're sleeping well. You will be glad you did this.

SLEEP TRAINING PITFALLS

While there's no one-size-fits-all sleep training method that works for everybody, there are some things that can either help or hinder your plan.

DOS	DON'TS
Start bedtime early. Waiting until your child is really sleepy often backfires. An overtired baby will be cranky and have a hard time soothing themselves.	Don't use electronic games or screens on phones or computers near bedtime. They're too stimulating and interfere with sleep.
Stay positive and supportive. Say, "Good night, sweetie. I'll see you tomorrow." Avoid apologizing, lingering, or making sad faces.	Don't rely on crutches to help your baby fall asleep, like holding them or rocking them to sleep, This will prevent your baby from learning independent sleep skills.
Expect this to take time. Most babies can be sleep trained at this age in about two weeks. It might take longer. Sleep (and crying!) may get worse before getting better, so stick with the plan.	Don't resume rocking or holding during middle-of-the-night awakenings. Instead, be consistent with your sleep plan at every awakening.

PLANNING BABY'S FIRST PARTY

You deserve a first birthday party! You've worked hard, and your baby has come a long way to reach this milestone. This first party is more for you and your partner than your baby, anyway. Sure, you'll want a few photos with family and friends, but remember, a big, noisy crowd is not going to be fun for the little one. They aren't going to get much personal satisfaction over opening presents. A small, relaxing party is best. Here are a few tips to making their first party one you'll remember:

→ Pick a time that's likely to work. Not during naptime.

→ Have extra hands at the ready. You may need help with cleaning, distracting, or taking your baby someplace quieter when they need a break.

→ Rather than having your baby dive into a big cake, you'll probably have a smaller "smash cake" for them to destroy. Note: You may be scraping colorful icing out of their ears for days.

→ You can reserve a restaurant or play space, but your child will be more comfortable at home and near their usual crib for a nap. Simple is best.

Dr. Knows Best: When to Stop Breastfeeding

The American Academy of Pediatrics encourages nursing for one year and leaves the timing of weaning up to what works best for each family. Some mothers and babies enjoy nursing and want to proceed longer, which is fine. But it's also okay for women to say, "I've had enough. I'd like to wean now." This is a personal decision that you can help your partner make by being supportive and open-minded.

WEANING BABY FROM BREAST OR BOTTLE

Some babies will wean on their own, losing interest in the breast or bottle as they approach 12 months. If that's your baby, it's usually best to let them take the lead and roll with it. Other babies might need a gentle push.

Wean breastfed babies onto a bottle if they're less than about 12 months; wean older babies directly to a cup. Wean bottle-fed babies to a cup at about 12 months. Whether coming from a breast or bottle background, the following tips will help:

Stop bedtime milk. Though it's a hard habit to break, breastfeeding or bottle-feeding before bedtime may prevent your baby from sleeping through the night. It's also bad for their teeth. Change the bedtime routine to not end with a feeding.

Partners, step in. Breastfed babies may refuse to take a bottle from your partner, but you, Dad, might be able to use a bottle when your partner is away.

Start cups early. Offer a sippy cup of water with every solid meal. Once they are about 12 months old, offer your baby milk from a cup at snacks and breakfast and water from a cup at lunch and dinner.

Go slow. Many babies do better if you substitute one weaned feeding (bottle or cup) for breastfeeding every few days, allowing babies to adjust before dropping another bottle or nursing. For nursing moms, going slow helps minimize breast engorgement and discomfort.

Or go fast! You know your baby best. Some babies wean fine off a bottle overnight. If that's the case, just throw the bottles out and offer only cups after the first birthday. For nursing babies, the fastest way is for Mom and partner to go on a three-day vacation away from baby. This can be uncomfortable for Mom if she still has a rich supply of milk, so it's best to use this method after interest in nursing has already dwindled.

INTRODUCING SOCIAL GESTURES

Your baby can communicate without words using social gestures. These are waves and claps that have a definite, and sometimes universal, meaning. Practice and teach these to your baby. It's rewarding and fun!

"Bye-bye." Babies catch this gesture, often one of the first, by watching and copying you. So start early, and use a "wave bye-bye" with your baby. At around 9 to 10 months, they may start waving back. Sometimes that wave happens after you leave rather than as you leave, so you might hear about it later.

"Pick me up." Babies will start to reach up to you with both arms when they want to be picked up. Make sure to add phrases like "You want to be picked up?" or "You want to come with Dad?" as you reach for them.

"Shaking head." The head shake is a universal gesture to mean "no." You might not even realize you're doing it. When you say "no," shake your head, and your baby will copy the movement to mean the same thing. Often, the "no" head shake comes before the word. Nodding the head up and down to mean "yes" is actually a more difficult skill that usually emerges when your child is older.

"Clap." Often accompanied by "Yay!" clapping means "You did good!" or "I'm happy," and it's a fun early gesture for babies to learn by copying you.

"Touchdown!" Is the Superbowl coming up? Teach your baby the two hands up touchdown gesture. ("Personal foul" is a trickier gesture for advanced babies.)

THE EMERGENCY DIAPER

It's going to happen. You'll be out with your baby, maybe at a friend's place or the mall, and you'll realize you're out of diapers. Maybe you forgot to restock the diaper bag, or maybe you left it at home. But have no fear. With a little ingenuity, you can save the day! Give these steps a try:

1. Find a diaper substitute, ideally something absorbent. Maybe a burp cloth, a small blanket or towel, a pillowcase, or a concert T-shirt from a band you no longer like. Choose something you won't mind throwing away later.

2. Find a safe space to lay your baby down where they won't roll.

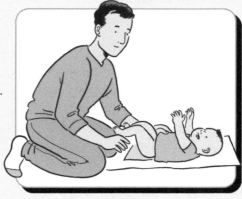

3. Remove baby's clothes and soiled diaper, and dispose of the diaper (see page 50).

4. Attach your diaper substitute with safety pins or duct tape, or just cover it with pants and hope for the best.

USING AN OPEN CUP

At this point, you're probably using a sippy cup for water. A sippy cup is an unbreakable plastic cup with a lid and a small spout that mimics drinking from a regular open cup. They sometimes have side handles.

Now's a good time to introduce the next drinking step: giving baby a regular, ordinary cup, just like the one you use. You'll have more mess at first, but using a cup is a great skill for your baby to master. It helps teach them how to use their hands, arms, and mouth all at once. Here are some tips for success:

Choose a cup that's sized for little hands. A smaller cup also means less mess when most of the contents inevitably hits their face and the floor. It should be made of unbreakable, dishwasher-safe plastic.

Start with water. Plain tap water is fine. Don't introduce milk in an open cup until they've mastered the skill of using the cup. Don't introduce juice or sweet drinks until they ask for it politely, by name. (e.g., "Daddy, may I please have some juice?")

Start small. Just an inch or so of water in the cup is plenty.

Model what they should do. You should drink from the same cup. Put water in it. Lift it with both hands, take a drink, and smack your lips in satisfaction.

Start outside. It's best to practice this out in the yard in warm weather. In the bathtub is also okay, but don't encourage your child to drink bathwater.

Dr. Knows Best: The Key to Healthy Eating

The most significant nutritional issue facing our children is overnutrition: eating too much and becoming overweight. The best way for parents to prevent this is to help their children develop their own independent eating habits. Offer your child healthy food and let them decide how much to eat. Don't push, encourage, or reward eating more. Let your child eat until they lose interest. This fosters a healthy outlook on eating and appetite that will last a lifetime.

SELF-FEEDING

When babies start to eat solids (around four to six months of age), they don't have the hand control to feed themselves. But by now, your child should be doing this on their own. It's a great way to practice hand-eye coordination. It also allows your child to experience different textures before putting them in their mouth, preventing negative reactions and gagging. Self-feeding is a crucial step toward independence. Embrace the mess and let your baby dig in!

Self-feeding should be part of a family meal. Sit with your child while (ideally) both you and your partner eat.

Resist the temptation to help. Your baby should use their own hands to put food in their mouth. Let them copy your motions and do it independently.

Resist the temptation to clean up until the meal is completely over. Yes, it's messy, but wiping their face is going to annoy and discourage them.

Any offered foods should be in small, hand-friendly morsels. Picture a single cooked kidney bean, a small cube of cooked carrot, or a little bit of scrambled egg. To prevent choking, everything should be smaller than the last knuckle on your baby's thumb.

Food should be squishable. Try a bit of meatball or meat loaf. Any cooked veggies, cooked pasta, egg, soft bread, or soft fruit is fine. If you're eating it and can squish it between your fingers, it's fine for your baby.

DEVELOPMENTAL GAMES

By now, your baby wants more interaction, surprises, exploration, and "cause and effect" adventures during playtime. The following are some great ideas to get started, but anything can become a learning game, so find what works for your child. Whatever you do, keep talking, singing, explaining, and moving!

→ **Bang a gong:** Got two objects? Bang them together! See what they sound like, both quiet and loud.

→ **Dance party:** Either use background tunes or sing yourself. If your back starts hurting after bending over to hold your baby's hand while they sit or stand, move to your knees.

→ **Sock puppets:** There are few bigger laughs you'll get than when you attack your baby's tummy with a sock puppet while saying, "Nom, nom, nom!"

→ **Stacking:** Almost anything can stack: plastic food containers, boxes of cereal, big chunky wooden or plastic blocks. Make towers together, then knock them down!

→ **Pouncing tiger:** Start with your baby some distance away and crawl toward them. Say, "Here comes the tiger!" Then roar and pounce! With time, your baby will try to escape, and that's part of the fun. Switch this around once your baby gets the hang of it.

→ **Bouncing fun:** You'll need a spare mattress or couch cushion. Have your baby stand in the middle (support them if needed), and help them crouch, jump, and bounce.

→ **Obstacle course:** Make one out of couch cushions and strategically placed furniture. Encourage your child to climb or walk over, around, or on it.

HIDE-AND-SEEK, INFANT EDITION

Infants love games involving hiding and finding. It's a way for them to learn object permanence ("Even if I can't see it, it's still there."), memory ("I remember where it is!"), and excitement ("You found it!"). There are a lot of variations that work well at this age:

Hide yourself: This is a form of peekaboo where you duck behind a piece of furniture or under a blanket. Say, "Where is Daddy?" to give your baby a clue.

Hide a toy: While your child is watching, take a blanket and put it over a toy. Then let them find it. Make it easier at first by letting some of the toy peek out. Feel free to wear a cape and call yourself a magician; then be surprised when your baby "ruins" your disappearing act. You can also hide things under cups, your hands, or in closed boxes.

Hide your baby: A big box works great, or under a coffee table or blanket. Then pretend to have trouble finding them. Look in several wrong places first to get some laughs.

Hide a snack: This is often done using a baby-safe breakfast cereal, like Cheerios. Hide them first under one clear cup, then one opaque cup. For advanced finders, try a three-card monte variation with three cups and one piece of cereal. Around and around they go, and where it is, nobody knows. When cereal is found, it gets eaten. Yum!

SCREEN TIME

Screen-based activities are part of our lives. They're entertainment, and they're also part of our jobs and education. But excessive screen time, or access to screen time too early in life, can get in the way of other developmental activities. Early screen time has also been associated with obesity, poor communication skills, and interference with sleep. Currently, the AAP discourages the use of all screen media for children younger than 18 months. The only exception is live (synchronous) video chatting with friends and family (like FaceTime with Grandpa).

Completely avoiding screens may be unrealistic for many families. They're everywhere! The negative impact of screen time can be reduced by:

• Limiting time in front of the screen, typically to less than 30 minutes a day.
• Choosing high-quality, age-appropriate material.
• Watching and interacting with the show or game together, asking questions, pointing, and sharing (just like you would if you were reading a book together).

Whatever you decide, remember that what you do sets an example. If you're frequently using your smartphone, your baby will notice and want to copy you. Read a magazine or take them outside to play. Enjoy your time with your fast-growing baby without your phone in your hand.

WATER FUN AND SAFETY

Babies and toddlers love water games like splashing in puddles, floating things in the tub, and pouring water into and out of containers. But they don't yet understand how dangerous water can be. Here's how to keep water play fun and safe:

Keep your baby away from water most of the time. You can't always supervise, so make sure pools are fenced, toilets are closed, and bathrooms are blocked. Outside doors must be kept closed to keep your baby from heading to the birdbath or outdoor puddles and ponds.

Empty water containers. Buckets, wading or kiddie pools, ice coolers, large pet bowls, or trash bins can all contain enough water to drown a child.

When it's time for water play, supervise. "Touch supervision" means when your baby is in or near a tub, swimming pool, or any container of water that's open, you should be able to easily reach and touch them without moving.

During this time, you must watch your baby. Don't get distracted by your phone or other people around you. Even if there's a lifeguard, you're on duty, too. If you must step away, take your child with you.

Consider swimming lessons. Recent evidence shows that even for young babies, formal swim instruction can offer another layer of protection. You

should especially look into swimming lessons if you have or live near a pool, but they're great for everyone. Remember, a young child who's had swimming lessons can still drown and must be supervised.

POINTING AND SHARING

One communication skill your baby is developing around this age is both simple and crucial to their future learning and development: using a finger to point, directing someone's attention to something else. As your baby develops, they'll begin to understand that a point doesn't mean "Look at my hand," but rather, "Look at that thing over there." And once you and your child can point and direct each other's attention to different things, an explosion of learning will occur. Here are some ways to encourage and use pointing gestures:

You point, then name it and talk about it. As you talk about things with your baby, point and show them what you mean. "That's a stop sign, it's red and means stop and hold still."

Baby points, you name it and talk about it. Look out for this, and reward and reinforce it when it starts to happen. Your baby will point at something, and that's your cue to name it and talk about it. "You're right, that's a cat," "That's where we go to get ice cream," or "That's a weird-looking potato!"

Baby points and you give it to them. Your baby will point at things to ask for them. As long as it's something safe, reward your pointer by handing it over, and name it while you're doing it. "You want your cup? Here's your cup!"

Dr. Knows Best: Laugh Together

How do you know you're doing the right thing with your baby? Are you playing the right games, giving the right feedback, and supporting your baby's development in the right way? Here's one simple rule of thumb: If your baby is happy and having fun, you're doing the right thing. And you should be having fun, too. Find games and activities that make you both laugh, and I guarantee you're on the right track.

HAVE FUN AND BE YOURSELF

The best activities to share are ones you and your baby both enjoy. Are you into sports? Bat balloons at each other. Are you creative? Finger paint and make up stories. A hiker? Take your baby along! Your baby should be part of the fun things that you like to do. You'll be a better dad by sharing what you love best. Here are a few more ideas for dads of any stripe. Try all of these. You might surprise yourself with a new hobby.

Ball sports: Use a beach ball or foam ball to roll toward each other, batting it across the floor. Help your baby dunk it in a laundry basket, kick it, throw it, or use it to knock things over.

Sprinkler fun: On a warm day, play in the grass with a water sprinkler. Add a tag-style game or soap bubbles to blow and chase.

Nature hunt: Explore and find whatever you can. Turn over rocks to find cool things. Collect sticks, make leaf piles, and toss mulch under the hedges. Teach your baby the difference between a crow and a blackbird. Collect bugs and frogs, then set them free.

Roadway: Use masking tape to create roadways on your floors, up your sofa, and anywhere else. Push cars around, figure out which car is fastest, and explain why you'll expect your baby to learn to drive a manual transmission. And then go outside with a bucket of suds and wash your wheels, together.

You can do just about anything you like to do with your baby. The best way to be the best dad is to have fun together!

Books

My Child Won't Sleep: A Quick Guide for the Sleep-Deprived Parent by Sujay Kansagra. A practical guide with many options on sleep training to fit different styles of parents and kids.

The Superkids Activity Guide to Conquering Every Day by Dayna Abraham. A fun guide that keeps kids busy and learning.

Vaccines: What Everyone Needs to Know by Kristen A. Feemster. An authoritative, complete, and reliable vaccine guide for parents.

Websites

CPR & First Aid
CPR.Heart.org
Every parent should learn CPR, and this is the place to start.

Diaper Free Baby
DiaperFreeBaby.org
For parents who are highly motivated and wish to raise their babies with no diapers at all, it can be done. This site has good instructions and support for the method called elimination communication.

Healthy Children

HealthyChildren.org

Authored by the American Academy of Pediatrics (AAP), the material on this site covers topics such as child safety, oral health, nutrition, media use, and much more, all with the definitive backing of the largest organization of pediatricians in the United States.

Immunization Action Coalition

Immunize.org

Written for parents, this in-depth site is kept carefully up-to-date and can answer just about any question about vaccines. Always science-based, it relies only on the best evidence from definitive sources.

La Leche League International

www.LLLI.org

This organization's website provides information, advice, and support to breastfeeding mothers.

Lemon Lime Adventures

LemonLimeAdventures.com

This blog and resource site focuses on younger children with behavioral or sensory problems and includes a lot of ideas for developmental play.

Precious Little Sleep

PreciousLittleSleep.com

This website with accompanying support group, books, and discussions presents friendly, practical, and realistic ways to help your baby (and you!) get a good night's sleep.

References

Abraham, Dayna. "Cloud Dough: Experimenting with Perfection." Accessed September 1, 2020. LemonLimeAdventures.com/cloud-dough-experiment.

American Academy of Pediatric Dentistry. "Oral Health Policies & Recommendations (The Reference Manual of Pediatric Dentistry)." Accessed September 1, 2020. AAPD.org/research/oral-health-policies--recommendations.

American Academy of Pediatrics. "Amount and Schedule of Formula Feedings." Accessed September 3, 2020. HealthyChildren.org/English/ages-stages/baby/formula-feeding/Pages/Amount-and-Schedule-of-Formula-Feedings.aspx.

American College of Obstetricians and Gynecologists. "Postpartum Depression." Accessed September 22, 2020. ACOG.org/patient-resources/faqs/labor-delivery-and-postpartum-care/postpartum-depression.

American Optometric Association. "Infant Vision: Birth to 24 Months of Age." Accessed September 10, 2020. AOA.org/healthy-eyes/eye-health-for-life/infant-vision.

Blair, Peter S., et al. "Bed-Sharing in the Absence of Hazardous Circumstances: Is There a Risk of Sudden Infant Death Syndrome? An Analysis from Two Case-Control Studies Conducted in the UK." PLOS ONE, September 19, 2014. doi.org/10.1371/journal.pone.0107799.

Centers for Disease Control and Prevention. "Infant and Toddler Nutrition." Accessed September 22, 2020. CDC.gov /nutrition/infantandtoddlernutrition/index.html.

Hagan, J. F., J. S. Shaw, and P. M. Duncan, eds. *Bright Futures: Guidelines for Health Supervision of Infants, Children, and Adolescents*. 4th ed. Elk Grove Village, IL: American Academy of Pediatrics, 2017.

National Highway Traffic Safety Administration. "Child Safety." Accessed September 1, 2020. NHTSA.gov/road-safety /child-safety.

Task Force on Sudden Infant Death Syndrome. "SIDS and Other Sleep-Related Infant Deaths: Updated 2016 Recommendations for a Safe Infant Sleeping Environment." *Pediatrics*, November 2016. doi.org/10.1542/peds.2016-2938.

Index

Acknowledgments

My best teachers have been my own kids. We grew, together.
I am proud of who you are and looking forward to who
you'll become.

I also want to thank the thousands of children and
their parents who've chosen me as their pediatrician.
I know parenting is hard. I hope we've had a chance to
share a laugh.

And thank you to my adorable and crazy-smart wife,
my partner and the mom of my kids. I couldn't have done
any of this without you.

About the Author

 **Roy Benaroch, MD,** has been in
practice as a general pediatrician
for more than 20 years and is on
the faculty of Emory University
School of Medicine. This is his
third book for parents. He's also
written and produced audio and
video courses on medical topics
for both medical professionals and
the general public. His blog, *The
Pediatric Insider*, has had more than 5 million views since
its inception in 2008. Find out more at RoyBenaroch.com.